The Art

Of

Winning

"Proven Techniques for Success in Business and Life"

SETH N. TAYLOR

Copyright

© [SETH N. TAYLOR] [2023]

All rights reserved. No part of this book may be reproduced, distributed, or transmitted in any form or by any means, including photocopying, recording, or other electronic or mechanical methods, without the prior written permission of the author, except in the case of brief quotations embodied in critical reviews and certain other noncommercial uses permitted by copyright law. For permission requests, please contact the author through.

DEDICATION

To everyone out there in the battle field of life and thriving for Success, this book is dedicated to you.

ACKNOWLEDGEMENT

I wish acknowledgement my business partners, team members, family.

You all contributed to the success of this life changing master piece.

Thank you.

Contents

Copyright 2

DEDICATION 3

ACKNOWLEDGEMENT 4

CHAPTER ONE 7

Introduction to the Art of Winning 7

CHAPTER TWO 28

Setting Clear Goals 28

CHAPTER THREE 45

Developing Effective Strategies 45

CHAPTER FOUR 67

Building Strong Relationships 67

CHAPTER FIVE 88

Mastering Self-Discipline 88

CHAPTER SIX 110

Embracing Change and Adaptability 110

CHAPTER SEVEN 131

Harnessing the Power of Creativity 131

CHAPTER EIGHT 151

Building Resilience and Perseverance 151

CHAPTER NINE 173

Effective Leadership Principles 173

CHAPTER TEN 197

Mastering Negotiation Skills 197

CHAPTER ELEVEN 222
Achieving Work-Life Balance 222
CHAPTER TWELVE 246
Leveraging Technology for Success 246
CHAPTER THIRTEEN 272
Financial Strategies for Success 272
CHAPTER FOURTEEN 306
Continuous Learning and Growth 306
CHAPTER FIFTEEN 328
Sustaining Success and Leaving a Legacy 328
ABOUT THE AUTHOR 351

CHAPTER ONE

Introduction to the Art of Winning

In the vast tapestry of human existence, there exists a ceaseless pursuit for triumph and accomplishment, a quest that transcends boundaries and resonates within the hearts of individuals from all walks of life. We yearn for the secrets that unlock the door to success, the alchemy that transforms dreams into reality, and the roadmap that guides us towards the pinnacle of achievement.

Welcome to "The Art of Winning: Proven Techniques for Success in Business and Life," a profound exploration into the very essence of triumph and the intricate dance between strategy and serendipity. Within these pages, you will embark on a transformative journey, uncovering the keys to unlock your full potential and propel yourself towards unprecedented heights.

Drawing from the wisdom of visionaries, titans of industry, and fearless trailblazers, this book offers a treasure trove of time-tested techniques, indispensable lessons, and unyielding motivation. Whether you are an aspiring entrepreneur seeking to carve your path through the competitive landscape of business, a professional longing to excel in your career, or an individual craving a profound sense of personal fulfillment, this book is your compass, pointing you towards the life you've always dreamed of.

From mastering the art of effective communication and building robust networks, to harnessing the power of resilience and embracing failure as a stepping stone to success, "The Art of Winning" leaves no stone unturned in its relentless pursuit of excellence. You will discover the subtle nuances of strategic decision-making, the unwavering determination required to overcome obstacles, and the transformative impact of cultivating a mindset geared towards victory.

But this book is not a mere collection of abstract principles and theoretical frameworks. It is a living, breathing tapestry of real-life stories, intimate anecdotes, and powerful examples that bring the lessons to life, infusing them with vibrancy and relatability. Through the pages of "The Art of Winning," you will meet extraordinary individuals who have faced adversity head-on, conquered insurmountable odds, and emerged victorious, their tales igniting the fire within you to take action and create your own success story.

Prepare to be challenged, inspired, and empowered as you traverse the extraordinary landscape of "The Art of Winning." The path may be arduous, but the rewards are immeasurable. The time has come to unleash the champion within, and with this book as your guide, the art of winning shall become your greatest ally in the pursuit of triumph in both business and life.

1.1 Understanding Success

Understanding success is a multifaceted concept that varies from person to person. It is often associated with achieving goals, reaching desirable outcomes, and experiencing fulfillment in various aspects of life, including business and personal endeavors. "The Art of Winning: Proven Techniques for Success in Business and Life" provides valuable insights into the principles and techniques that can contribute to one's success.

To truly understand success, it is crucial to recognize that it goes beyond mere material wealth or societal recognition. Success encompasses a holistic approach that encompasses both professional and personal aspects of life. It involves finding a sense of purpose, setting meaningful goals, and making consistent progress towards their attainment.

One key aspect of success lies in self-awareness and understanding one's own strengths, weaknesses, passions, and values. By recognizing their unique attributes, individuals can align their pursuits with their innate talents and inclinations. This self-awareness allows individuals to identify their areas of expertise and leverage them to their advantage, leading to a higher probability of success.

Another important aspect emphasized in "The Art of Winning" is the power of perseverance and resilience. Success rarely comes easily or without obstacles. It requires tenacity and the ability to bounce back from failures and setbacks. Viewing setbacks as opportunities for growth and learning, rather than insurmountable roadblocks, is essential for long-term success.

Moreover, success is often intertwined with effective goal setting and strategic planning. Setting clear, specific, and achievable goals provides a roadmap for success, helping individuals stay focused and motivated. By breaking down larger objectives into smaller, manageable tasks, individuals can maintain a sense of progress and momentum, which is instrumental in achieving long-term success.

Furthermore, success is not solely an individual pursuit. It is often fostered within supportive networks and communities. Building and nurturing meaningful relationships with mentors, colleagues, and like-minded individuals can provide guidance, support, and valuable opportunities. Collaboration and the ability to leverage the strengths of others can significantly enhance one's chances of success.

Lastly, success is closely tied to a growth mindset. Embracing a mindset of continuous learning, adaptability, and open-mindedness is crucial for staying relevant and seizing new opportunities. Successful individuals understand that change is inevitable, and they actively seek out new knowledge and skills to adapt to evolving circumstances.

In conclusion, understanding success requires a comprehensive approach that goes beyond mere financial achievements. It involves self-awareness, perseverance, strategic planning, meaningful relationships, and a growth mindset. "The Art of Winning: Proven Techniques for Success in Business and Life" offers valuable insights and techniques to navigate the complex journey towards success, enabling individuals to unlock their full potential and lead fulfilling lives.

1.2 The Role of Strategy

The role of strategy plays a vital part in achieving success, both in business and in life. Strategy is the art of formulating a plan of action to achieve specific goals or objectives. It involves making conscious choices about how resources will be allocated, what actions will be taken, and how various factors will be managed to reach the desired outcome. The implementation of a well-crafted strategy can significantly increase the likelihood of success by providing a roadmap for decision-making, resource allocation, and problem-solving.

In business, a well-defined strategy serves as a guide for organizations to navigate the complex and competitive landscape. It helps in identifying the direction the company should take, determining the market segment to target, and outlining the steps to be taken to gain a competitive advantage. A clear strategy enables businesses to allocate their resources efficiently, prioritize initiatives, and make informed decisions that align with their long-term vision. It also provides a framework for adapting to changing market conditions and seizing opportunities as they arise.

Strategy is not limited to the corporate world alone. It also plays a crucial role in personal and professional development. In life, having a strategy helps individuals set meaningful goals, identify the steps needed to achieve them, and make deliberate choices to reach their desired outcomes. A personal strategy can include aspects such as career planning, financial management, health and wellness goals, and personal relationships. By having a clear strategy, individuals can focus their efforts, make informed decisions, and overcome obstacles along the way.

A well-developed strategy provides several benefits. It enhances clarity and focus, ensuring that individuals and organizations are aligned with their objectives. Strategy also promotes effective resource allocation by identifying areas of strength and weakness, allowing for efficient use of time, money, and effort. It helps in minimizing risks by anticipating potential challenges and developing contingency plans. Moreover, strategy facilitates innovation and adaptability, enabling individuals and organizations to stay ahead of the curve and respond effectively to changing circumstances.

However, it is essential to note that strategy is not a one-time exercise. It requires continuous evaluation and adaptation as circumstances evolve. Strategies need to be flexible enough to accommodate unforeseen challenges and opportunities, and regular review and adjustment are necessary to ensure ongoing effectiveness.

In conclusion, strategy plays a fundamental role in achieving success in both business and life. It provides a framework for decision-making, resource allocation, and problem-solving. A well-defined strategy enhances clarity, focus, and efficiency, enabling individuals and organizations to navigate complex environments and achieve their goals. By embracing strategy as a guiding principle, one can significantly increase the chances of success and fulfillment in various aspects of life.

1.3   Cultivating a Winning Mindset

In the pursuit of success, one fundamental aspect that sets apart high achievers from the rest is their mindset. A winning mindset is not merely a stroke of luck or an inherent trait; it is a conscious choice and a deliberate practice. By adopting certain proven techniques, individuals can cultivate a winning mindset that empowers them to achieve their goals, overcome obstacles, and thrive in both business and life.

First and foremost, cultivating a winning mindset requires a strong sense of self-belief. Believing in oneself and one's abilities is the foundation upon which success is built. This involves recognizing and capitalizing on personal strengths while acknowledging areas for improvement. By embracing a growth mindset, individuals understand that failures and setbacks are stepping stones to growth and learning. They view challenges as opportunities for self-improvement and are not deterred by temporary setbacks.

Another essential element of a winning mindset is maintaining a positive attitude. Positivity breeds resilience and fuels determination. It is crucial to approach obstacles and difficulties with optimism, reframing them as challenges to be conquered rather than insurmountable roadblocks.

Embracing a positive mindset also entails surrounding oneself with like-minded individuals who inspire, motivate, and encourage personal growth.

Additionally, successful individuals cultivate a strong sense of purpose and set clear, achievable goals. A clear vision provides direction and clarity, guiding actions towards desired outcomes. By setting measurable and realistic goals, individuals can break them down into smaller, manageable steps, fostering a sense of progress and accomplishment. Celebrating each milestone along the way reinforces the belief in one's ability to achieve even greater success.

Persistence is another key characteristic of a winning mindset. The path to success is rarely linear, and setbacks are inevitable. However, those with a winning mindset view obstacles as opportunities to develop resilience and tenacity. They remain committed to their goals, persevere through challenges, and never lose sight of the bigger picture.

Moreover, cultivating a winning mindset involves embracing continuous learning and self-improvement. Successful individuals are avid seekers of knowledge, constantly seeking new insights and skills that can propel them forward. They invest in personal development, whether through reading, attending seminars, or seeking mentorship. This thirst for knowledge ensures they stay ahead of the curve, adapt to changing circumstances, and seize opportunities as they arise.

Lastly, gratitude plays a significant role in a winning mindset. Recognizing and appreciating the present moment, along with past accomplishments, fosters a sense of fulfillment and contentment. Gratitude also fuels motivation, as it reminds individuals of their capabilities and the support they have received along their journey.

In conclusion, cultivating a winning mindset is a conscious choice that requires consistent effort and practice. It encompasses self-belief, positivity, goal-setting, persistence, continuous learning, and gratitude. By adopting these proven techniques, individuals can transform their mindset, unlocking their full potential, and achieving success in both business and life.

CHAPTER TWO

Setting Clear Goals

2.1 Defining Success

Success can be defined as the achievement of a desired outcome or the attainment of a goal. It is a deeply personal and subjective concept that varies from individual to individual. When it comes to setting clear goals and defining success, it is essential to articulate what you want to accomplish without using the word "by." Instead of focusing on time constraints or external factors, it is important to concentrate on the essence of success itself.

Defining success involves envisioning the desired end result or the state you want to reach. It is about identifying the specific outcomes or milestones that will mark your progress and give you a sense of accomplishment. By setting clear goals, you can establish a roadmap towards success and create a framework for your actions and decisions.

To define success, consider the following approaches:

a) **Clarity of Purpose:** Define success by clarifying the purpose behind your goals. Ask yourself why you want to achieve a particular outcome. Understand the underlying motivations, values, and aspirations that drive you. Success can be defined as aligning your actions with your purpose and living a meaningful life.

b) **Personal Growth:** Success can be viewed as continuous personal growth and development. It is about expanding your knowledge, skills, and capabilities. Set goals that challenge you, push your limits, and enable you to become the best version of yourself. Success is the ongoing process of learning, improving, and evolving.

c) **Impact and Contribution:** Define success by the impact you make on others and the world around you. Consider the positive influence you can have on individuals, communities, or even the global scale. Success can be measured by the difference you make and the contributions you offer to society.

d) **Emotional Well-being:** Success is not solely about external achievements; it also encompasses your emotional well-being and fulfillment. Define success by the level of happiness, contentment, and satisfaction you experience in different aspects of your life. It involves nurturing relationships, maintaining a healthy work-life balance, and prioritizing self-care.

e) **Resilience and Adaptability:** Success can be defined by your ability to overcome challenges, adapt to change, and bounce back from setbacks. Focus on developing resilience and embracing a growth mindset. Define success as the journey of overcoming obstacles, learning from failures, and persisting in the face of adversity.

Remember, defining success is a deeply personal process. It is crucial to set goals that align with your values, passions, and aspirations. By defining success in a way that resonates with you, you can stay motivated, focused, and empowered to achieve your goals and create a fulfilling life.

2.2 SMART Goal Setting

SMART goal setting is a popular framework used to set clear and achievable objectives. The acronym SMART stands for Specific, Measurable, Attainable, Relevant, and Time-bound. It provides a structured approach to goal setting that increases the likelihood of success. Here's an explanation of each component of SMART goal setting:

a) **Specific:** A goal should be specific and well-defined. It should answer the questions: What do I want to accomplish? Why is it important? Who is involved? Where will it take place? The more specific the goal, the clearer the direction and the better the chances of achieving it.

b) **Measurable:** Goals should be measurable, meaning that they can be quantified or observed. Setting measurable goals helps in tracking progress and determining whether the goal has been achieved. By using concrete metrics or indicators, you can evaluate your progress objectively.

c) **Attainable:** Goals should be realistic and attainable. While it's important to set ambitious goals, they should still be within reach. Assess your available resources, skills, and time to ensure that the goal is attainable. Setting goals that are too far out of reach may lead to frustration and demotivation.

d) **Relevant:** Goals should be relevant and aligned with your overall objectives. They should be meaningful and contribute to your personal or professional growth. Consider how the goal aligns with your values, aspirations, and long-term plans. Setting relevant goals ensures that your efforts are focused on what truly matters.

e) **Time-bound:** Goals should have a specific timeframe or deadline. Setting a timeline creates a sense of urgency and helps you prioritize tasks accordingly. It also allows you to track your progress and make necessary adjustments along the way. A deadline provides a sense of accountability and helps prevent procrastination.

By following the SMART framework, you can increase your chances of setting clear, actionable goals that are more likely to be achieved. Remember that goal setting is an ongoing process, and it's essential to regularly review and adjust your goals as circumstances change.

2.3 Creating an Action Plan

Define your objectives: Start by clearly defining your goals. What do you want to achieve? Be specific and ensure that your goals are measurable, attainable, relevant, and time-bound (SMART). For example, instead of saying, "Increase sales," specify, "Increase monthly sales revenue by 10% within the next six months."

a) **Break it down:** Once you have identified your main goal, break it down into smaller, manageable tasks or milestones. These smaller objectives will help you stay focused and provide a roadmap for reaching your ultimate goal. Each task should contribute directly to the accomplishment of your main objective.

b) **Prioritize:** Determine the order in which you need to tackle your tasks. Consider the dependencies between tasks and identify which ones need to be completed before others can begin. Prioritizing will help you allocate your time and resources efficiently and ensure that you are working on the most critical tasks first.

c) **Assign responsibilities:** Clearly assign responsibilities to individuals or teams for each task. Ensure that everyone understands their role and what is expected of them. By assigning responsibilities, you promote accountability and ensure that progress is being made on all fronts.

d) **Set deadlines:** Establish realistic deadlines for each task. Deadlines create a sense of urgency and help maintain momentum. Make sure the deadlines align with your overall timeline for achieving your main goal. However, be careful not to set unrealistic or overly tight deadlines that may lead to unnecessary stress or compromised quality of work.

e) **Determine resources:** Identify the resources required to complete each task successfully. This may include personnel, tools, equipment, or financial resources. Assess what is available and plan for any additional resources that may be needed. Adequate resource allocation ensures that your action plan is feasible and supports the achievement of your goals.

f) **Monitor progress:** Regularly track and monitor the progress of each task. Use measurable indicators to assess whether you are on track or if adjustments need to be made. This allows you to identify any bottlenecks, address issues promptly, and make necessary course corrections to ensure you're moving towards your goal effectively.

g) **Communicate and collaborate:** Foster open communication and collaboration within your team or stakeholders. Regularly update them on progress, challenges, and successes. Encourage feedback and ensure that everyone understands the overall goal and their individual contributions. Effective communication and collaboration enhance teamwork and increase the likelihood of achieving your goals.

h) **Evaluate and adapt:** Once you have completed your action plan, evaluate the overall outcome. Assess the effectiveness of your approach, identify what worked well, and areas for improvement. Learn from the experience and use these insights to refine your future goal-setting and action planning processes.

Remember, setting clear goals is crucial, but without a well-defined action plan, it can be challenging to achieve them. By following these steps, you can create an effective action plan that provides structure, accountability, and a roadmap to success.

CHAPTER THREE

Developing Effective Strategies

3.1 Analyzing the Competitive Landscape

Analyzing the competitive landscape is a critical step in developing effective strategies for any organization. It involves identifying and evaluating the strengths, weaknesses, opportunities, and threats posed by competitors in the market. This analysis provides valuable insights that can help businesses make informed decisions and gain a competitive edge. Here are some key aspects to consider when analyzing the competitive landscape:

a) **Identify Competitors:** Start by identifying the direct and indirect competitors in your industry. Direct competitors offer similar products or services to the same target market, while indirect competitors may have different offerings but still compete for the same customer base.

b) **Assess Market Share:** Determine the market share of each competitor to understand their relative position and influence in the industry. This information can be obtained through market research, industry reports, or publicly available data.

c) **Evaluate Competitive Advantage:** Analyze the unique strengths and advantages of each competitor. This includes factors such as pricing strategies, product differentiation, brand reputation, customer loyalty, distribution channels, and technological capabilities. Understanding what sets competitors apart can help you identify areas where you need to improve or find opportunities to differentiate your own offering.

d) **SWOT Analysis:** Conduct a comprehensive SWOT (Strengths, Weaknesses, Opportunities, Threats) analysis for each competitor. Assess their strengths and weaknesses in terms of product quality, marketing, operations, financial resources, and human capital. Identify the opportunities they are capitalizing on and the threats they face, such as new market entrants, regulatory changes, or emerging technologies.

e) **Monitor Industry Trends:** Stay updated on the latest industry trends, market shifts, and consumer preferences.

This can be done through market research, industry publications, attending trade shows or conferences, and leveraging digital tools and social media platforms. Understanding the evolving landscape will enable you to anticipate changes and adapt your strategies accordingly.

f) **Customer Insights:** Gain insights into customer preferences, behaviors, and satisfaction levels by conducting customer surveys, focus groups, or analyzing online reviews and social media conversations. Understanding what customers value and how your competitors are meeting those needs can inform your own strategic decisions.

g) **Benchmarking:** Compare your organization's performance and capabilities against competitors using key performance indicators (KPIs). This benchmarking exercise helps identify performance gaps and areas for improvement.

h) **Competitive Intelligence:** Gather intelligence on your competitors' activities, such as product launches, pricing changes, marketing campaigns, partnerships, and expansion plans. This information can be obtained through various sources, including industry reports, news articles, public financial statements, and online monitoring tools.

i) **Anticipate Competitive Responses:** Consider how your competitors might react to your own strategic moves. This includes analyzing their likely responses to price changes, product innovations, or market entry. By anticipating their actions, you can proactively plan countermeasures or prepare for potential competitive threats.

j) **Collaborative Opportunities:** Explore collaborative opportunities with competitors, such as partnerships, joint ventures, or industry alliances. While they may be rivals in some areas, there could be mutually beneficial opportunities to leverage each other's strengths or combine resources for shared goals.

Analyzing the competitive landscape provides valuable insights for developing effective strategies. By understanding the strengths and weaknesses of competitors, market trends, and customer preferences, organizations can make informed decisions, differentiate themselves, and gain a competitive advantage in the marketplace.

3.2 Identifying Key Success Factors

Identifying key success factors is a crucial step in developing effective strategies for any endeavor, whether it's in business, personal goals, or any other area of life. Key success factors are the critical elements that significantly contribute to achieving desired outcomes and objectives. By identifying these factors, you can focus your efforts and resources on the most impactful areas, increasing your chances of success. Here are some steps to help you identify key success factors:

a) Clearly define your goals and objectives:

Start by clarifying what you want to

achieve. Whether it's launching a new product, increasing market share, or personal development, having well-defined goals will provide a framework for identifying the factors that will contribute to your success.

b) **Conduct a SWOT analysis:** Perform a comprehensive analysis of your strengths, weaknesses, opportunities, and threats (SWOT). Assessing your internal strengths and weaknesses will help you identify areas where you have a competitive advantage or areas that need improvement. Additionally, analyzing external opportunities and threats will uncover factors in the market or industry that could impact your success.

c) **Analyze industry and market trends:** Stay up-to-date with the latest trends, innovations, and changes in your industry or market. Look for factors that have a significant impact on success, such as customer preferences, technological advancements, regulatory changes, or competitive dynamics. Understanding these trends will help you identify the factors that are critical to staying competitive and achieving your goals.

d) **Study successful examples:** Research and analyze successful organizations or individuals in your field. Identify common factors that have contributed to their success. This can include factors such as a strong brand reputation, exceptional customer service, efficient operations, or unique value propositions. Learning from others' successes can provide valuable insights into the key factors that drive achievement.

e) **Gather feedback and insights:** Engage with stakeholders who have a vested interest in your success. This includes customers, employees, partners, and industry experts. Conduct surveys, interviews, or focus groups to gather their perspectives and insights. This feedback can help you identify factors that are crucial to meeting their needs and expectations.

f) **Prioritize and validate key factors:** Once you have identified potential success factors, prioritize them based on their impact and relevance to your goals. Test and validate these factors by analyzing data, conducting experiments, or seeking expert opinions. This process will help you refine your understanding and ensure that you focus on the most critical elements.

g) **Continuously monitor and adapt:** Keep in mind that success factors may change over time due to evolving market conditions, technological advancements, or shifting customer preferences. Regularly monitor the environment and reassess your key success factors to ensure they remain relevant and aligned with your goals.

By diligently identifying key success factors, you can develop effective strategies that leverage your strengths, mitigate weaknesses, capitalize on opportunities, and navigate potential threats. These factors will serve as guideposts to direct your efforts, allocate resources effectively, and increase your chances of achieving your desired outcomes.

3.3 Crafting Winning Strategies

Developing effective strategies is crucial for organizations to achieve their goals and gain a competitive advantage in today's dynamic business environment. Crafting winning strategies requires careful analysis, thoughtful planning, and the ability to adapt to changing circumstances. Here are some key considerations for creating successful strategies:

a) **Clear Vision and Goals:** A winning strategy begins with a clear vision of what the organization aims to achieve. This vision should be supported by well-defined goals that are specific, measurable, achievable, relevant, and time-bound (SMART). By having a clear direction, the organization can align its resources and efforts towards a common objective.

b) **External and Internal Analysis:** To craft a winning strategy, it is essential to conduct a thorough analysis of the external environment and internal capabilities. This involves understanding the industry dynamics, identifying market trends, assessing competitors, and evaluating the organization's strengths and weaknesses. By gaining insights into these factors, you can identify opportunities to capitalize on and mitigate potential threats.

c) **Differentiation and Competitive Advantage:** A winning strategy should focus on creating a unique value proposition and differentiation in the market. This involves identifying the organization's core competencies and leveraging them to gain a competitive advantage. Whether it's through product innovation, superior customer service, cost leadership, or other means, differentiation is key to standing out in a crowded marketplace.

d) **Target Market and Segmentation:** Understanding the target market and effectively segmenting customers is essential for crafting winning strategies. By identifying specific customer groups with distinct needs and preferences, organizations can tailor their offerings and marketing strategies to better meet those requirements. This targeted approach allows for more efficient resource allocation and higher customer satisfaction.

e) **Flexibility and Adaptability:** In today's rapidly changing business landscape, strategies must be flexible and adaptable. Successful organizations continuously monitor the external environment, stay abreast of market trends, and adjust their strategies accordingly. This may involve seizing new opportunities, responding to competitive threats, or adapting to emerging technologies. The ability to pivot and embrace change is critical for long-term success.

f) **Implementation and Execution:** Crafting a winning strategy is only the first step; successful implementation and execution are equally important. This requires effective communication, resource allocation, and the alignment of activities across different functions and departments. Establishing clear milestones, setting performance metrics, and regularly reviewing progress are vital to ensure strategy implementation stays on track.

g) **Continuous Learning and Improvement:** Strategies should not be set in stone. Organizations must foster a culture of continuous learning and improvement. This involves regularly evaluating strategy outcomes, collecting feedback, and making necessary adjustments. By embracing a learning mindset, organizations can stay ahead of the curve and adapt to evolving market conditions.

In conclusion, crafting winning strategies is a dynamic and ongoing process that requires a deep understanding of the external environment, internal capabilities, and customer needs. By having a clear vision, leveraging differentiation, being adaptable, and executing effectively, organizations can develop strategies that drive success and create a sustainable competitive advantage.

CHAPTER FOUR

Building Strong Relationships

4.1 The Power of Networking

In today's interconnected world, networking has become an essential skill for personal and professional growth. Networking involves actively creating and nurturing relationships with individuals who share similar interests, goals, or professional fields. It goes beyond exchanging business cards at events; it's about building meaningful connections that can open doors to new opportunities, collaboration, and support. The power of networking lies in its ability to facilitate personal and professional growth, providing individuals with a strong foundation for success.

Expanding Opportunities:

Networking opens doors to a world of opportunities that might otherwise remain inaccessible. By connecting with people from diverse backgrounds and industries, you expose yourself to new ideas, perspectives, and potential collaborations. Through networking, you can discover career opportunities, job openings, or partnerships that can propel your professional growth.

Building a strong network can serve as a catalyst for discovering uncharted territories and accessing resources that can enhance your success.

Knowledge Sharing and Learning:

Networking allows you to tap into the wealth of knowledge and experiences possessed by others. By engaging in conversations and discussions with individuals from different fields, you gain insights, information, and expertise that can broaden your horizons. Networking events, conferences, and online communities provide platforms to learn from experts, engage in thought-provoking discussions, and stay updated with the latest trends and innovations in your industry. Networking becomes a two-way street, where you contribute and receive knowledge, fostering continuous learning.

Building Lasting Relationships:

One of the most significant advantages of networking is the ability to build genuine and lasting relationships. Connections made through networking can evolve into valuable friendships, mentorships, or partnerships. These relationships are built on trust, mutual support, and shared interests. Strong relationships formed through networking can provide guidance, advice, and a support system during both professional and personal challenges. People within your network become a reliable source of information, referrals, and recommendations, enabling you to navigate through various situations with confidence.

Boosting Confidence and Visibility:

Networking helps individuals develop essential interpersonal skills, such as communication, active listening, and relationship building. Regularly engaging with others and sharing your ideas in networking settings helps boost your confidence in expressing yourself and articulating your thoughts. As you build a reputation within your network, you become more visible and recognized for your expertise, skills, and contributions. Increased visibility can lead to new opportunities, speaking engagements, or invitations to collaborate on projects, further enhancing your professional growth.

Overcoming Challenges and Adversities:

Networking provides a support system during challenging times. Whether you face a career setback, a professional dilemma, or simply need advice, your network can offer guidance and assistance. The diverse perspectives and experiences within your network can provide valuable insights and alternative solutions to the challenges you encounter. Moreover, networking allows you to connect with individuals who have overcome similar obstacles, providing inspiration and motivation to persevere.

The power of networking lies in its ability to build strong relationships, expand opportunities, foster knowledge sharing, boost confidence, and provide a support system. It transcends traditional networking events and encompasses meaningful connections made with individuals who share common interests or professional goals. By actively investing time and effort into networking, you can unlock a wealth of possibilities and create a solid foundation for personal and professional growth. So, seize the power of networking and embrace the opportunities it presents on your journey to success.

4.2 Building Trust and Rapport

Building trust and rapport is crucial for establishing and maintaining strong relationships, whether they are personal or professional. Trust forms the foundation of any healthy relationship, and rapport helps to foster a deeper connection and understanding between individuals. Here are some key principles and strategies to consider when it comes to building trust and rapport:

- **Open and Honest Communication:** Effective communication is essential for building trust and rapport. Be transparent, share your thoughts and feelings, and actively listen to the other person. Create an environment where open dialogue is encouraged, and make sure that both parties feel heard and understood.

- **Reliability and Consistency:** Consistently following through on your commitments and being reliable builds trust. Be punctual, deliver on your promises, and demonstrate a consistent pattern of behavior. This reliability shows others that they can depend on you and trust your word.

- **Respect and Empathy:** Treat others with respect and empathy, recognizing their perspectives and emotions. Show genuine interest in their experiences and validate their feelings. By being understanding and compassionate, you create a safe space where trust and rapport can flourish.

- **Shared Values and Integrity:** Establishing common values and demonstrating integrity helps build trust. Align your actions with your words and principles, and be transparent about your values. When both parties share similar values and can trust each other's integrity, it strengthens the foundation of the relationship.

- **Building Emotional Connections:** Connect with others on an emotional level. Show empathy, express vulnerability, and share experiences. This emotional connection deepens rapport and fosters a sense of trust and understanding.

- **Conflict Resolution:** Conflicts are inevitable in any relationship, but how you handle them can either strengthen or weaken trust and rapport. Approach conflicts with a problem-solving mindset, listen to different perspectives, and find mutually beneficial solutions. Resolving conflicts in a fair and respectful manner helps build trust and rapport.

- **Consistent Support:** Be there for others consistently, especially during challenging times. Offer your support, provide encouragement, and demonstrate that you genuinely care about their well-being. Being a consistent source of support builds trust and strengthens the bond between individuals.

- **Authenticity:** Be yourself and encourage others to be authentic as well. Authenticity creates a sense of trust because it shows that you are genuine and sincere. Embrace vulnerability, share your thoughts and emotions honestly, and encourage others to do the same.

Remember that building trust and rapport takes time and effort. It requires consistent application of these principles and a genuine desire to create meaningful connections. By investing in trust and rapport, you can cultivate strong and lasting relationships in both your personal and professional life.

4.3 Effective Communication Skills

Effective communication skills are essential for building strong relationships, whether in personal or professional settings. Clear and efficient communication not only helps in expressing thoughts and ideas accurately but also fosters understanding, trust, and collaboration among individuals. Here are some key aspects to consider when it comes to developing effective communication skills:

- **Active Listening:** Listening is a crucial component of effective communication. Practice active listening by giving your full attention to the speaker, maintaining eye contact, and showing genuine interest. Avoid interrupting or formulating responses in your mind while the other person is speaking. By truly listening, you can better understand the message being conveyed and respond appropriately.

- **Clarity and Conciseness:** Clear and concise communication eliminates ambiguity and ensures that your message is understood correctly. Use simple and straightforward language, avoiding jargon or technical terms that may confuse others. Organize your thoughts before speaking or writing, and focus on delivering your message in a concise manner to prevent information overload.

- **Non-Verbal Communication:** Non-verbal cues, such as facial expressions, gestures, and body language, play a significant role in communication. Be mindful of your own non-verbal signals and pay attention to those of others. Maintain good posture, use appropriate hand gestures, and establish eye contact to convey interest and openness. Aligning your non-verbal communication with your spoken words can enhance the clarity and impact of your message.

- **Empathy and Emotional Intelligence:** Effective communication involves understanding and empathizing with others. Try to put yourself in the other person's shoes and consider their perspective. Show empathy by acknowledging their emotions and validating their experiences. Emotional intelligence enables you to navigate conversations with sensitivity and handle difficult situations with tact and understanding.

- **Feedback and Clarification:** Feedback is crucial for effective communication. Encourage open and honest feedback from others, and be open to receiving constructive criticism. When unsure about something, ask for clarification to ensure you have understood the message accurately. By seeking feedback and clarifying information, you can minimize misunderstandings and promote effective communication.

- **Adaptability and Flexibility:** Communication styles vary among individuals, and it's important to adapt your approach accordingly. Pay attention to the communication preferences of others and adjust your style to accommodate different personalities and situations. Flexibility allows for better collaboration and understanding, leading to stronger relationships.

- **Conflict Resolution:** Effective communication skills are particularly valuable in resolving conflicts. When disagreements arise, practice active listening, remain calm, and choose your words carefully. Focus on finding common ground and seeking a solution that benefits all parties involved. Constructive communication during conflicts helps in preserving relationships and fostering growth.

Remember that effective communication is a skill that can be developed with practice and self-awareness. By continually honing your communication skills, you can build stronger relationships, promote understanding, and achieve success in various aspects of life.

CHAPTER FIVE

Mastering Self-Discipline

5.1   Overcoming Procrastination

Procrastination is a common struggle that many people face when it comes to completing tasks and achieving their goals. It is the act of delaying or postponing tasks, often due to a lack of motivation, discipline, or a tendency to prioritize short-term gratification over long-term benefits. While it may provide temporary relief, procrastination ultimately hinders personal growth, productivity, and success.

Overcoming procrastination requires developing self-discipline and adopting effective strategies to manage and prioritize tasks. In this discussion, we will explore some key techniques to help you overcome procrastination and become more self-disciplined.

- **Understand the underlying causes:** Procrastination often has deeper psychological roots. It may be triggered by fear of failure, perfectionism, overwhelm, lack of clarity, or a lack of intrinsic motivation. Identifying the specific reasons behind your procrastination tendencies can help you address them directly.

- **Set clear goals:** Having clear, well-defined goals is crucial in combating procrastination. Break down your larger goals into smaller, manageable tasks. When you have a clear plan of action, it becomes easier to stay focused and motivated.

- **Prioritize tasks:** Not all tasks are equally important or urgent. Learn to prioritize your tasks based on their significance and deadlines. This way, you can allocate your time and energy more effectively, ensuring that important tasks are completed on time.

- **Create a schedule:** Establishing a structured schedule can help you overcome procrastination. Set specific time slots for different activities and allocate sufficient time for each task. Stick to your schedule as much as possible and make it a habit to start and finish tasks within the allotted time frame.

- **Break tasks into smaller steps:** Sometimes, the sheer magnitude of a task can be overwhelming and demotivating. Break tasks into smaller, more manageable steps. By focusing on one step at a time, you can make progress and build momentum, which will help overcome procrastination.

- **Practice the Pomodoro Technique:** The Pomodoro Technique is a time management method that involves working in focused, uninterrupted blocks of time, typically 25 minutes, followed by short breaks. This technique can enhance your productivity and help you avoid distractions, reducing the tendency to procrastinate.

- **Eliminate distractions:** Identify and eliminate potential distractions that hinder your productivity. This could include turning off notifications on your phone, closing unnecessary browser tabs, or finding a quiet, dedicated workspace. Minimizing distractions creates an environment conducive to concentration and focus.

- **Use positive reinforcement:** Rewarding yourself after completing tasks can be a powerful motivator. Set up a system of rewards for yourself, whether it's a small treat, a break, or doing something you enjoy. Celebrating your achievements reinforces positive behavior and encourages you to continue overcoming procrastination.

- **Develop self-discipline:** Self-discipline is a skill that can be developed over time. Start by setting small, achievable goals and consistently working towards them. As you build momentum and witness the positive results of your efforts, your self-discipline will strengthen.

- **Cultivate motivation and inspiration:** Find ways to stay motivated and inspired throughout your journey. This could involve reading motivational books, listening to podcasts, surrounding yourself with supportive and like-minded individuals, or visualizing your desired outcomes. Cultivating motivation helps counteract the urge to procrastinate.

Remember, overcoming procrastination requires consistent effort and practice. Be patient with yourself and recognize that setbacks may occur along the way. By implementing these strategies and maintaining a commitment to self-discipline, you can gradually overcome procrastination and unlock your full potential.

5.2 Developing Productive Habits

Developing productive habits is a key aspect of mastering self-discipline. When we cultivate habits that support our goals and values, we become more effective and efficient in our endeavors. Productive habits enable us to consistently make progress towards our objectives and ultimately lead to long-term success. In this response, I will elaborate on the process of developing productive habits and offer some practical strategies to facilitate this transformation.

- **Set Clear Goals:** To develop productive habits, it is crucial to have a clear understanding of what you want to achieve. Set specific, measurable, attainable, relevant, and time-bound (SMART) goals. Clearly defining your objectives provides a sense of direction and serves as a motivator to develop habits that align with those goals.

- **Start Small:** When adopting new habits, it's essential to start small and focus on gradual progress. Begin with one or two habits that are manageable and easy to incorporate into your routine. For example, if your goal is to become more physically active, start by committing to a 15-minute walk every day before gradually increasing the intensity and duration of your exercise routine.

- **Create a Routine:** Consistency is key when it comes to developing productive habits. Establish a daily routine that incorporates your desired habits. Having a regular schedule helps to automate actions, reducing the need for decision-making and willpower. As the saying goes, "We are what we repeatedly do." By embedding your productive habits into a routine, they become an integral part of your lifestyle.

- **Implement Habit Stacking:** Habit stacking is a technique that involves attaching a new habit to an existing one. Identify an existing habit that you already do consistently and link your new habit to it. For instance, if you want to read more books, you could decide to read ten pages every night before going to bed. By associating the new habit with an established one, you leverage the existing cue to trigger the desired behavior.

- **Track Progress:** Monitoring your progress is essential for maintaining motivation and accountability. Keep a record of your habit development journey. This can be done through journaling, using habit-tracking apps, or simply marking a calendar. Visualizing your progress provides a sense of accomplishment and encourages you to stay on track.

- **Practice Mindfulness:** Developing productive habits requires awareness and conscious effort. Cultivate mindfulness by being fully present in the moment and paying attention to your thoughts and actions. When you catch yourself engaging in unproductive behaviors or deviating from your desired habits, gently redirect your focus back to your goals. Mindfulness helps you stay focused, overcome distractions, and make intentional choices.

- **Seek Support and Accountability:** Surrounding yourself with like-minded individuals who share similar goals can significantly impact your habit development journey. Join communities or find an accountability partner who can provide support, encouragement, and constructive feedback. Sharing your progress and challenges with others not only helps you stay motivated but also provides fresh perspectives and insights.

- **Embrace Failure as a Learning Opportunity:** Developing productive habits is not always a linear process. It's normal to experience setbacks or occasional lapses. Instead of being discouraged by failures, view them as learning opportunities. Analyze what went wrong, adjust your approach if needed, and get back on track. Remember that self-discipline is built through persistence and resilience.

By implementing these strategies consistently, you can gradually transform your actions into productive habits that align with your goals. Keep in mind that developing productive habits is an ongoing process that requires patience and dedication. With time, effort, and self-discipline, you can create a life characterized by productivity, success, and personal fulfillment.

5.3 Managing Time Effectively

Managing time effectively is a fundamental aspect of mastering self-discipline. Time is a finite resource, and how we allocate and utilize it can greatly impact our productivity, success, and overall sense of fulfillment. By adopting effective time management strategies, individuals can optimize their daily routines, prioritize tasks, and achieve their goals more efficiently.

One of the key principles of managing time effectively is setting clear goals and objectives. Without a sense of direction, it becomes challenging to determine how to allocate time appropriately. By defining specific, measurable, attainable, relevant, and time-bound (SMART) goals, individuals can gain clarity on what they want to achieve and align their actions accordingly.

To effectively manage time, it is crucial to create a structured schedule or to-do list. Breaking down larger goals into smaller, manageable tasks helps in avoiding overwhelm and allows for better focus. It is beneficial to prioritize tasks based on their importance and urgency, ensuring that critical tasks are given precedence. Tools like calendars, planners, or digital task management applications can be utilized to organize and visualize the schedule effectively.

Additionally, individuals should aim to eliminate or minimize time-wasting activities. Procrastination, excessive use of social media, and other distractions can significantly hamper productivity. Recognizing and controlling these distractions is essential. Techniques such as the Pomodoro Technique, where work is broken down into focused intervals followed by short breaks, can help improve concentration and efficiency.

Another crucial aspect of time management is learning to delegate and outsource tasks when appropriate. It is often not feasible or efficient to handle everything independently. Delegating tasks to others who are better equipped or have more time available can free up valuable time for more important responsibilities.

Moreover, effective time managers understand the importance of maintaining a healthy work-life balance. Dedicate time for personal well-being, leisure activities, and relationships. Allowing oneself to relax and recharge helps prevent burnout and enhances overall productivity when it's time to work.

Furthermore, effective time managers regularly evaluate their progress and make adjustments as necessary. Reflecting on how time is being spent, identifying areas of improvement, and making necessary changes to the routine are essential for continuous growth and efficiency. This can involve reviewing the effectiveness of strategies, identifying time-consuming tasks that can be eliminated or streamlined, and seeking opportunities for personal and professional development.

In summary, managing time effectively is a critical component of mastering self-discipline. By setting clear goals, creating structured schedules, prioritizing tasks, eliminating distractions, delegating when necessary, maintaining work-life balance, and regularly evaluating progress, individuals can optimize their use of time and increase their productivity and success in various areas of life. With commitment and consistent practice, effective time management can become a habit that enhances overall self-discipline and personal fulfillment.

CHAPTER SIX

Embracing Change and Adaptability

6.1 The Importance of Agility

Agility is a crucial characteristic in today's rapidly changing world. It refers to the ability to swiftly and effectively respond to new circumstances, challenges, and opportunities. Embracing agility is essential for individuals, organizations, and societies to navigate the unpredictable nature of modern life. Whether it's adapting to technological advancements, shifting market trends, or unexpected disruptions, agility enables us to thrive in an ever-evolving landscape.

The importance of agility can be observed across various domains, including business, personal growth, and societal progress. In the business realm, agility is a fundamental factor for success. Companies that can quickly adapt to changing market conditions are more likely to stay competitive and meet the evolving needs of their customers. Agile organizations are adept at identifying emerging trends, anticipating customer preferences, and adjusting their strategies accordingly. By being responsive to market demands, they can seize new opportunities and maintain a sustainable advantage over their competitors.

Agility is equally valuable on an individual level. In today's dynamic work environment, where job roles are constantly evolving, being agile allows individuals to thrive and remain relevant. It entails being open to new ideas, continuously learning and upgrading one's skills, and embracing change with a positive mindset. Those who are agile are more likely to adapt to new technologies, industry shifts, and changing job requirements. They can seize career opportunities, navigate transitions with ease, and maintain a growth mindset that fosters personal and professional development.

Furthermore, in the face of unexpected disruptions, agility becomes even more critical. Disruptive events such as economic downturns, natural disasters, or global pandemics can significantly impact individuals, organizations, and entire societies. Being agile enables us to respond swiftly and effectively to such crises, minimizing the negative impact and bouncing back stronger. Agile individuals can quickly identify alternative paths, embrace innovative solutions, and display resilience in the face of adversity. Similarly, agile organizations can pivot their operations, restructure their processes, and adapt their business models to ensure survival and future growth.

Agility is also closely tied to innovation. By being agile, individuals and organizations create an environment that encourages experimentation, embraces failure as a learning opportunity, and fosters a culture of continuous improvement. The ability to adapt and respond flexibly to changing circumstances often leads to innovative ideas and solutions. Agile individuals and organizations are more likely to challenge the status quo, think outside the box, and explore new possibilities. This, in turn, drives progress and enables them to stay ahead in an ever-evolving world.

In conclusion, the importance of agility cannot be overstated in today's fast-paced and uncertain world. Embracing agility allows individuals, organizations, and societies to effectively respond to change, seize opportunities, and thrive in a constantly evolving landscape. It enables businesses to stay competitive, individuals to remain relevant in their careers, and societies to navigate disruptions with resilience. By fostering agility, we can unlock innovation, embrace change, and build a future that is adaptable, dynamic, and filled with possibilities.

6.2 Thriving in Dynamic Environments

Thriving in dynamic environments requires embracing change and adaptability. In today's fast-paced world, the only constant is change, and those who can effectively navigate and harness the power of change are the ones who thrive. Whether it's in the workplace, personal life, or society at large, the ability to adapt and embrace change is essential for success.

To thrive in dynamic environments, one must first develop a mindset that welcomes change as an opportunity for growth. Instead of fearing change or resisting it, individuals who embrace it see it as a chance to learn, explore new possibilities, and expand their horizons. They understand that change brings fresh perspectives, innovative ideas, and the potential for personal and professional development.

Adaptability is a crucial skill in thriving in dynamic environments. It involves being open-minded, flexible, and willing to adjust one's approach or strategies when faced with new circumstances or challenges. Adaptable individuals possess a willingness to unlearn and relearn, to let go of old habits or ways of thinking that may no longer be effective. They actively seek new knowledge and skills, continuously improve themselves, and readily embrace new technologies or methodologies.

Another key aspect of thriving in dynamic environments is being proactive rather than reactive. Instead of waiting for change to happen, individuals who thrive actively seek out opportunities for growth and progress. They anticipate potential changes and trends, stay informed, and position themselves to take advantage of emerging opportunities. They are proactive in identifying potential risks and challenges, and they develop contingency plans to mitigate them effectively.

Effective communication is also critical in thriving in dynamic environments. As change often involves collaboration with others, being able to communicate clearly, listen actively, and build strong relationships becomes paramount. Individuals who thrive in dynamic environments are adept at conveying their ideas, thoughts, and concerns effectively, and they are also receptive to feedback and different perspectives.

Resilience is another vital trait in thriving in dynamic environments. Change can be disruptive and challenging, and setbacks or failures are inevitable. However, resilient individuals bounce back from adversity, learn from their experiences, and use setbacks as stepping stones to future success. They view challenges as opportunities to test their abilities, build their resilience muscle, and emerge stronger.

Furthermore, a growth mindset is closely intertwined with thriving in dynamic environments. Those with a growth mindset believe in their ability to learn and develop, seeing challenges as opportunities for growth rather than fixed limitations. They embrace a love for lifelong learning and continuously seek ways to expand their knowledge and skills.

Lastly, embracing diversity and inclusion is crucial for thriving in dynamic environments. Diversity brings different perspectives, experiences, and ideas, fostering innovation and creativity. Inclusive environments value and respect the contributions of individuals from diverse backgrounds, creating a culture that is adaptable and open to change.

In summary, thriving in dynamic environments requires embracing change and adaptability. It involves developing a mindset that welcomes change as an opportunity for growth, being adaptable and proactive, communicating effectively, cultivating resilience and a growth mindset, and embracing diversity and inclusion. By embracing these principles, individuals can navigate the ever-changing landscape with confidence, seize opportunities, and achieve personal and professional success in dynamic environments.

6.3 Turning Challenges into Opportunities

Turning challenges into opportunities is a mindset and approach that embraces change and adaptability. It is the ability to see potential in difficult situations and transform them into favorable outcomes. Rather than being overwhelmed or discouraged by obstacles, individuals and organizations with this mindset actively seek out ways to navigate through challenges and leverage them as catalysts for growth and progress.

One of the key aspects of turning challenges into opportunities is adopting a positive and proactive attitude. Instead of viewing challenges as roadblocks, individuals with this mindset see them as chances to learn, improve, and innovate. They understand that adversity often brings out the best in people, fostering creativity, resilience, and problem-solving skills.

When facing a challenge, the first step is to assess the situation objectively. This involves understanding the root causes, potential consequences, and available resources. By analyzing the challenge from different perspectives, one can identify underlying opportunities that may have been hidden at first glance. This critical thinking process allows for a more strategic and effective approach to tackling the problem.

Next, embracing change requires flexibility and adaptability. It means being open to new ideas, alternative solutions, and different ways of doing things. This mindset allows individuals to adjust their strategies and tactics in response to changing circumstances. By being flexible, they can seize unexpected opportunities that arise during the course of overcoming challenges.

Turning challenges into opportunities often involves taking calculated risks. It requires stepping out of one's comfort zone and exploring uncharted territory. Taking risks can lead to growth and innovation, as it encourages experimentation and learning from both successes and failures. This willingness to take risks is essential for capitalizing on opportunities that may have otherwise been missed.

Moreover, collaboration and networking play a crucial role in transforming challenges into opportunities. By connecting with others who have complementary skills and knowledge, individuals can leverage collective expertise to overcome obstacles. Collaborative efforts can lead to the discovery of new perspectives, innovative solutions, and potential partnerships that can turn challenges into mutually beneficial opportunities.

In addition, continuous learning and self-improvement are vital for embracing change and adaptability. By staying informed about emerging trends, technologies, and best practices, individuals can anticipate challenges and proactively prepare for them. Continuous learning enables individuals to acquire new skills, expand their knowledge base, and enhance their problem-solving abilities, enabling them to seize opportunities as they arise.

Lastly, maintaining a growth mindset is essential in the process of turning challenges into opportunities. A growth mindset entails believing in one's ability to learn and develop, even in the face of setbacks. It involves seeing challenges as stepping stones rather than obstacles, understanding that failures are learning experiences, and persisting in the pursuit of goals despite difficulties. By embracing a growth mindset, individuals can unlock their full potential and maximize the opportunities that come their way.

In conclusion, turning challenges into opportunities requires a combination of mindset, skills, and actions. It involves adopting a positive and proactive attitude, embracing change and adaptability, taking calculated risks, collaborating with others, continuously learning, and maintaining a growth mindset. By approaching challenges with this perspective, individuals and organizations can transform adversity into growth, innovation, and success.

CHAPTER SEVEN

Harnessing the Power of Creativity

7.1 Nurturing Innovation

Nurturing innovation is the process of creating an environment that fosters and encourages the development of new and creative ideas. It involves providing individuals and teams with the resources, support, and freedom to explore and experiment, thereby unleashing their potential for generating groundbreaking solutions and inventions. By fostering innovation, organizations can stay ahead in today's rapidly evolving and competitive landscape.

There are several key elements to consider when nurturing innovation:

a) Culture of Creativity: Building a culture that values and promotes creativity is crucial. This involves encouraging open communication, collaboration, and the sharing of ideas without fear of judgment or failure. Leaders need to foster an atmosphere that embraces risk-taking and rewards innovative thinking.

b) Empowerment and Autonomy: Providing individuals with a sense of ownership and autonomy over their work is essential. When employees have the freedom to explore and experiment with their ideas, they are more likely to take risks and come up with innovative solutions. Empowering them with decision-making authority and resources to pursue their ideas encourages a sense of ownership and accountability.

c) Cross-functional Collaboration: Encouraging collaboration across different departments and teams can lead to the exchange of diverse perspectives and knowledge. When individuals from different backgrounds and areas of expertise come together, they can leverage their unique insights to spark creativity and find novel solutions. This interdisciplinary approach can break down silos and promote a culture of innovation.

d) Continuous Learning and Development: Investing in employee training and development is crucial for nurturing innovation. By providing opportunities for individuals to enhance their skills, learn new technologies, and stay updated with industry trends, organizations create an environment that supports ongoing learning and intellectual growth. This continuous learning mindset enables employees to think beyond conventional boundaries and find innovative solutions to complex challenges.

e) Supportive Infrastructure and Resources: Providing the necessary infrastructure, tools, and resources is essential for nurturing innovation. This includes allocating budgets for research and development, providing access to cutting-edge technologies, and creating physical spaces that facilitate collaboration and creativity. Organizations should also establish processes for idea generation, evaluation, and implementation, ensuring that innovative ideas can be effectively harnessed and transformed into tangible outcomes.

f) Recognition and Rewards: Recognizing and rewarding innovative efforts is vital to sustain a culture of innovation. Celebrating both small and significant achievements creates a positive feedback loop that encourages individuals and teams to continue pushing boundaries and exploring new possibilities. Reward mechanisms can include financial incentives, promotions, public acknowledgment, or even dedicated innovation awards within the organization.

g) Embracing Failure as a Learning Opportunity: Innovation inherently involves taking risks, and not all ideas will succeed. Nurturing innovation requires a mindset that sees failure as an opportunity for learning and growth. Encouraging individuals to learn from their failures, share their experiences, and iterate on their ideas fosters a culture of resilience and continuous improvement.

By focusing on these key elements, organizations can create an environment that nurtures innovation and unleashes the power of creativity. By fostering a culture that supports and rewards innovation, organizations can drive breakthrough discoveries, develop competitive advantages, and adapt to the ever-changing demands of the market.

7.2 Thinking Outside the Box

Thinking outside the box is a popular concept that encourages individuals to approach problems and challenges from innovative and unconventional perspectives. It refers to the ability to break free from traditional and conventional thinking patterns in order to generate fresh ideas and find creative solutions. This approach requires individuals to explore new possibilities, challenge existing assumptions, and embrace a mindset that goes beyond the limits of conventional wisdom.

When someone thinks outside the box, they venture beyond the confines of established norms and standard practices. They question the status quo and are willing to explore uncharted territories. This type of thinking can be applied to various areas of life, including business, art, science, and personal development. It enables individuals to tap into their creativity, imagination, and problem-solving abilities in order to come up with unconventional and often groundbreaking ideas.

One of the key aspects of thinking outside the box is the ability to question assumptions. Often, our thinking is limited by preconceived notions, biases, and beliefs that we have accepted as truth. By challenging these assumptions and looking at things from a different angle, we can discover new perspectives and possibilities that were previously hidden. This requires a willingness to take risks and embrace uncertainty, as thinking outside the box often involves venturing into unfamiliar territory.

Another important element of thinking outside the box is the ability to connect seemingly unrelated ideas or concepts. This is often referred to as "associative thinking" or "lateral thinking." By making unexpected connections between different domains or disciplines, individuals can generate innovative ideas and solutions. This requires a broad knowledge base and a willingness to explore diverse areas of interest. It also involves being open-minded and receptive to ideas from different sources, as well as being curious and inquisitive about the world around us.

In order to cultivate a mindset of thinking outside the box, it is important to foster an environment that encourages and supports creativity and innovation. This can be done by promoting a culture of openness, where ideas are valued regardless of their source or initial feasibility. It also involves creating spaces for brainstorming and idea generation, where individuals can freely express their thoughts and explore unconventional approaches. Additionally, embracing failure as a learning opportunity and encouraging experimentation can help individuals overcome the fear of taking risks and enable them to push the boundaries of conventional thinking.

Thinking outside the box is not a skill that comes naturally to everyone, but it can be developed and honed with practice. It requires individuals to break free from their comfort zones, challenge their own assumptions, and embrace uncertainty. By doing so, they can tap into their innate creativity and unlock new possibilities. Whether it's solving complex problems, creating innovative products, or exploring new artistic expressions, thinking outside the box is a powerful tool that can lead to remarkable achievements and groundbreaking discoveries.

7.3 Problem-Solving Strategies

Problem-solving strategies are essential tools that enable individuals and organizations to tackle challenges, overcome obstacles, and find innovative solutions. Harnessing the power of creativity within problem-solving strategies can significantly enhance the effectiveness and efficiency of these approaches. By incorporating creative thinking into problem-solving, individuals can generate fresh perspectives, break free from conventional patterns of thought, and discover novel solutions that may have otherwise remained hidden.

One prominent problem-solving strategy that emphasizes creativity is known as "divergent thinking." Divergent thinking involves exploring a wide range of possibilities, generating multiple ideas, and embracing unconventional or non-linear approaches. This strategy encourages individuals to think beyond the obvious and traditional solutions, opening up new avenues for exploration.

To effectively employ divergent thinking, several techniques can be employed. One such technique is brainstorming, which involves a group of individuals freely sharing ideas without any criticism or judgment. Brainstorming sessions often encourage participants to think outside the box and build upon each other's suggestions, fostering a collaborative and creative problem-solving environment.

Another technique is mind mapping, which allows individuals to visually organize and connect ideas. By creating a graphical representation of the problem and its potential solutions, mind mapping enables individuals to identify relationships, uncover hidden connections, and explore alternative pathways. This technique leverages the brain's natural inclination to make associations, facilitating a more creative problem-solving process.

Creativity can also be fostered through the "lateral thinking" problem-solving strategy. Lateral thinking involves approaching problems from unconventional angles, challenging assumptions, and exploring alternative perspectives. This strategy encourages individuals to ask thought-provoking questions, consider different viewpoints, and employ techniques such as analogy and metaphor to generate innovative solutions.

Moreover, the SCAMPER technique is another creative problem-solving strategy that can be applied. SCAMPER is an acronym representing seven different methods of modifying or transforming a problem: Substitute, Combine, Adapt, Modify, Put to another use, Eliminate, and Reverse. Each element prompts individuals to think creatively about how they can change or transform aspects of the problem to generate new ideas and solutions.

Additionally, design thinking, a human-centered problem-solving approach, incorporates creativity throughout the entire problem-solving process. Design thinking involves empathizing with users, defining the problem, ideating potential solutions, prototyping and testing, and iterating based on feedback. This iterative process encourages designers to continuously explore and refine ideas, leveraging their creative abilities to generate user-centric solutions.

In harnessing the power of creativity within problem-solving strategies, it is important to create an environment that nurtures and encourages innovative thinking. This includes fostering a culture that values and rewards creativity, providing resources and support for experimentation, and promoting collaboration and diverse perspectives. By embracing creativity and integrating it into problem-solving strategies, individuals and organizations can unlock new possibilities, overcome complex challenges, and drive meaningful innovation.

CHAPTER EIGHT

Building Resilience and Perseverance

8.1 Overcoming Setbacks and Failure

Overcoming setbacks and failure is an essential aspect of building resilience and perseverance. In life, we often encounter obstacles, face challenges, and experience failures that can shake our confidence and hinder our progress. However, it is through these setbacks that we have the opportunity to learn, grow, and ultimately become stronger individuals.

One of the first steps in overcoming setbacks and failure is to shift our mindset and view them as valuable learning experiences rather than insurmountable roadblocks. Failure should not be seen as a reflection of our worth or capabilities but rather as a stepping stone towards improvement. By adopting a growth mindset, we can approach setbacks with a sense of curiosity, embracing the lessons they offer and seeking opportunities for personal development.

When faced with a setback or failure, it is important to take the time to reflect on what went wrong and why. Self-reflection allows us to gain a deeper understanding of the situation, identify any mistakes or shortcomings, and explore alternative strategies or approaches. This introspection helps us avoid repeating the same errors in the future and enables us to develop a more effective plan moving forward.

Another crucial element in overcoming setbacks is resilience. Resilience is the ability to bounce back from adversity, to persevere in the face of challenges, and to maintain a positive attitude despite setbacks. Building resilience requires cultivating a strong belief in oneself and one's abilities. It involves developing emotional strength, adaptability, and the willingness to confront difficult situations head-on.

It is also important to seek support from others during times of setback or failure. Surrounding ourselves with a network of trusted individuals, such as friends, family, mentors, or colleagues, can provide emotional support, encouragement, and valuable insights. Their perspectives and experiences may offer new strategies or ideas to overcome obstacles and find a way forward. Moreover, sharing our struggles with others helps us realize that setbacks are a common part of life and that we are not alone in facing them.

Additionally, maintaining a positive mindset and focusing on the lessons learned from setbacks can significantly contribute to overcoming failure. It is natural to feel disappointed or discouraged when things don't go as planned, but dwelling on negativity only prolongs the recovery process. Instead, it is important to reframe the situation, emphasizing the opportunities for growth and personal development that arise from failure. By focusing on the positive aspects and visualizing success, we can regain our motivation and move forward with renewed determination.

Lastly, perseverance is key to overcoming setbacks and failure. It is the ability to stay committed to our goals and aspirations despite obstacles and setbacks along the way. Perseverance requires determination, patience, and a long-term perspective. It means not giving up at the first sign of difficulty but rather pushing through challenges, adapting to changing circumstances, and maintaining our focus on the ultimate objective. Embracing a never-give-up attitude can ultimately lead to success, even after multiple setbacks.

In conclusion, setbacks and failure are inevitable in life, but they provide us with opportunities for growth, learning, and building resilience. By adopting a growth mindset, reflecting on our experiences, seeking support, maintaining a positive outlook, and cultivating perseverance, we can overcome setbacks and use failure as a stepping stone towards future success. Embracing setbacks as valuable learning experiences allows us to bounce back stronger, more resilient, and better equipped to face future challenges.

8.2 Developing Mental Toughness

Developing mental toughness is a valuable skill that can greatly contribute to building resilience and perseverance in various aspects of life. Mental toughness refers to the ability to maintain a strong and resilient mindset, enabling individuals to overcome challenges, setbacks, and adversity. It involves cultivating a positive and unwavering attitude, managing stress effectively, and maintaining focus and determination in the face of obstacles. Developing mental toughness is a process that requires intentional effort and practice, but the benefits are well worth it.

Here are some key components and strategies for developing mental toughness:

Mindset and Attitude:

a) **Embrace a growth mindset:** Adopt the belief that challenges are opportunities for growth and learning. View setbacks as temporary obstacles that can be overcome with effort and perseverance.

b) **Cultivate optimism:** Focus on the positive aspects of situations and look for potential solutions instead of dwelling on problems. Maintain a hopeful and positive outlook, even in difficult times.

c) **Develop self-belief:** Build confidence in your abilities and trust in your capacity to handle challenges. Remind yourself of past successes and use them as a source of motivation.

Emotional Regulation:

a) **Practice self-awareness:** Be mindful of your emotions and thoughts. Recognize when negative emotions arise and take steps to manage them effectively.

b) **Reframe negative thinking:** Challenge and reframe negative thoughts or self-talk. Replace self-limiting beliefs with positive and empowering affirmations.

c) **Develop resilience to stress:** Engage in stress-management techniques such as deep breathing exercises, meditation, or physical activities to reduce stress levels and promote emotional well-being.

Goal Setting and Planning:

a) **Set specific and realistic goals:** Break down larger goals into smaller, manageable tasks. This provides a sense of accomplishment and progress, boosting motivation.

b) **Create a plan of action:** Develop a strategic plan that outlines the steps required to achieve your goals. Having a clear roadmap helps maintain focus and direction, even when faced with obstacles.

Perseverance and Grit:

a) **Stay committed:** Commit to your goals and values, even when the going gets tough. Remind yourself of the reasons behind your pursuits and the long-term benefits they offer.

b) **Embrace discomfort:** Recognize that growth and development often come from stepping outside of your comfort zone. Embrace challenges as opportunities for personal and professional advancement.

Learn from failures: View failures as learning experiences rather than personal setbacks. Extract lessons from setbacks, adjust your approach, and continue moving forward.

Support and Self-Care:

a) **Seek support:** Surround yourself with a supportive network of friends, family, or mentors who can provide guidance, encouragement, and perspective during challenging times.

b) **Practice self-care:** Prioritize self-care activities such as exercise, sufficient rest, healthy eating, and engaging in hobbies or activities that bring joy and relaxation. Taking care of your physical and mental well-being is essential for maintaining resilience.

Developing mental toughness is a continuous process that requires patience, perseverance, and a willingness to embrace discomfort. By cultivating a resilient mindset and adopting strategies to manage stress and setbacks, individuals can enhance their ability to persevere in the face of challenges and build a strong foundation for success in various areas of life.

8.3 Cultivating a Positive Mindset

Cultivating a positive mindset is a powerful tool for building resilience and perseverance in the face of challenges and setbacks. It involves training your mind to focus on the positive aspects of life, develop optimistic thinking patterns, and maintain a hopeful outlook even in difficult circumstances. By adopting a positive mindset, individuals can enhance their ability to overcome obstacles, bounce back from failures, and maintain a sense of motivation and determination. Here are some key aspects of cultivating a positive mindset:

a) **Awareness and Self-reflection:** Developing a positive mindset begins with self-awareness and reflection. Take time to observe your thoughts, emotions, and reactions to different situations. Notice any negative or self-limiting beliefs that may be holding you back. By becoming aware of these patterns, you can start to challenge and reframe them into more positive and empowering thoughts.

b) **Positive Self-Talk:** Pay attention to the way you talk to yourself. Replace self-criticism and negative self-talk with positive and affirming statements. Encourage and support yourself with kind and motivating words. Remind yourself of your strengths, past successes, and the progress you have made. By changing your inner dialogue, you can boost your confidence and resilience.

c) **Gratitude Practice:** Cultivating gratitude is an effective way to shift your focus towards the positive aspects of your life. Regularly practice gratitude by acknowledging and appreciating the things you have, the people in your life, and the experiences that bring you joy. Keep a gratitude journal or simply take a few moments each day to reflect on what you are grateful for. This practice helps to counterbalance negative thinking and fosters a positive outlook.

d) **Positive Surroundings:** Surround yourself with positive and supportive people who uplift and inspire you. Engage in activities and hobbies that bring you joy and fulfillment. Create a positive environment at home and work by incorporating elements that promote positivity, such as uplifting quotes, inspiring artwork, or calming music. Your surroundings can greatly influence your mindset and attitude.

e) **Embracing Failure as a Learning Opportunity:** Instead of viewing failures as setbacks, reframe them as opportunities for growth and learning. Embrace a mindset that sees failure as a natural part of the journey toward success. Analyze the lessons learned from each failure and use them to improve and make better decisions in the future. Adopting this perspective allows you to persevere through challenges and setbacks with resilience.

f) **Visualization and Positive Affirmations:** Use the power of visualization to create a positive mental image of your goals and desired outcomes. Imagine yourself succeeding, overcoming obstacles, and reaching your aspirations. Combine visualization with positive affirmations, which are positive statements about yourself and your abilities. Repeat these affirmations regularly to reinforce a positive mindset and boost self-confidence.

g) **Mindfulness and Stress Management:** Practice mindfulness to stay present and focused on the current moment. This helps reduce anxiety and worry about the past or future. Engage in stress management techniques like deep breathing, meditation, or physical exercise to release tension and promote a positive state of mind. Taking care of your physical and mental well-being is crucial for building resilience and maintaining a positive outlook.

Remember, cultivating a positive mindset is a continuous practice that requires consistency and effort. It may not always be easy, especially during challenging times, but with persistence and dedication, you can gradually shift your mindset towards positivity. By embracing a positive outlook on life, you can build resilience and perseverance to navigate through obstacles and achieve your goals.

CHAPTER NINE

Effective Leadership Principles

9.1 Inspiring and Motivating Others

Inspiring and motivating others is a crucial aspect of effective leadership. It involves creating a positive and engaging work environment where individuals feel empowered, enthusiastic, and driven to achieve their best. When leaders inspire and motivate their team members, they can unleash their full potential, increase productivity, and foster a culture of excellence and innovation. In this response, I will elaborate on some key principles and strategies for inspiring and motivating others as a leader.

1. **Lead by example:** As a leader, your actions speak louder than words. Your behavior and work ethic set the tone for your team. By consistently demonstrating dedication, integrity, and a strong work ethic, you inspire your team members to follow suit. When they see you taking on challenges, staying positive, and striving for excellence, they will be motivated to do the same.

2. **Clearly communicate goals and expectations:** People need to

understand what they are working towards and what is expected of them. Effective leaders clearly communicate the vision, goals, and expectations to their team members. By providing a clear direction and explaining the significance of their work, leaders inspire individuals to see the bigger picture and how their contributions make a difference.

3. **Provide meaningful feedback and recognition:** Regular feedback and recognition are essential for motivation. Leaders should provide constructive feedback to help individuals grow and

improve. Acknowledging and appreciating their efforts and achievements boosts morale and motivates team members to continue striving for excellence. Celebrating milestones and accomplishments reinforces a positive and rewarding work environment.

4. **Empower and delegate:** Effective leaders empower their team members by delegating meaningful responsibilities and trusting them to perform their tasks. By giving individuals autonomy and ownership over their work, leaders inspire confidence and motivate them to

take ownership and excel. Leaders should provide guidance and support, but also allow individuals to contribute their unique skills and ideas, fostering a sense of purpose and pride in their work.

5. **Foster a positive work culture:** A positive work culture is vital for motivation and inspiration. Leaders should promote open communication, collaboration, and teamwork. Encouraging a supportive and inclusive environment where everyone's ideas and opinions are valued fosters creativity and innovation. Creating opportunities for personal and professional growth,

such as training programs or mentorship, shows that you care about your team members' development and motivates them to invest in their own growth.

6. **Set realistic challenges and provide growth opportunities:** Humans are naturally driven by challenges and personal growth. Effective leaders provide their team members with meaningful challenges that push them out of their comfort zones while ensuring they have the necessary resources and support to succeed. By offering growth

opportunities, such as training, mentoring, or advancement possibilities, leaders inspire motivation by showing individuals that their efforts can lead to personal and professional development.

7. **Cultivate a positive work-life balance:** Recognizing the importance of work-life balance is essential for inspiring and motivating others. Leaders should encourage and support their team members in achicving a healthy balance between their personal and professional lives. This can include flexible work arrangements, promoting self-care practices, and recognizing the

importance of time off. When individuals feel supported in their well-being, they are more likely to be motivated, engaged, and productive at work.

In conclusion, inspiring and motivating others is a key responsibility of effective leaders. By leading by example, communicating goals, providing feedback and recognition, empowering and delegating, fostering a positive work culture, offering growth opportunities, and promoting work-life balance, leaders can create an environment where individuals feel motivated, inspired, and empowered to achieve their best. Such leadership practices not only benefit the individuals but also contribute to the overall success and growth of the organization.

9.2 Building High-Performing Teams

Building high-performing teams is a crucial aspect of effective leadership. A high-performing team is a group of individuals who come together with diverse skills, talents, and experiences to achieve a common goal. These teams are characterized by their ability to consistently deliver exceptional results, adapt to challenges, and collaborate effectively. Leaders play a pivotal role in creating an environment that fosters high performance and enables team members to reach their full potential. Here are some key principles for building high-performing teams:

1. Clear Vision and Goals: A leader must establish a clear and compelling vision for the team. This vision serves as a guiding light and aligns team members towards a common purpose. Alongside the vision, leaders need to define specific, measurable goals that provide a roadmap for the team's success. Clear goals help team members understand expectations and work together towards achieving them.

2. **Building a Diverse Team:** High-performing teams benefit from diversity in skills, perspectives, and backgrounds. A leader should actively seek out individuals with different strengths and experiences to create a well-rounded team. Diversity fosters innovation, creativity, and better problem-solving, as team members bring unique insights and approaches to the table.

3. **Effective Communication:** Communication is vital for team cohesion and success. A leader should establish open lines of communication, encourage transparency, and create a

safe environment where team members feel comfortable expressing their ideas, concerns, and feedback. Regular team meetings, one-on-one conversations, and utilizing various communication tools facilitate effective information exchange and collaboration.

4. **Building Trust:** Trust is the foundation of a high-performing team. Leaders must actively work to build trust among team members and between themselves and the team. Trust is cultivated through consistent actions, keeping promises, demonstrating integrity, and fostering a culture of

mutual respect. When team members trust each other and their leader, they are more likely to collaborate, take risks, and support one another.

5. **Empowering and Delegating:** A leader should empower team members by providing them with autonomy and authority to make decisions and take ownership of their work. Delegating tasks and responsibilities according to individual strengths and skills not only lightens the leader's workload but also empowers team members to showcase their abilities and grow professionally. This approach fosters a sense of

ownership and accountability within the team.

6. **Encouraging Collaboration and Synergy:** Collaboration is essential for high-performing teams. A leader should encourage an environment of cooperation, where team members feel encouraged to share knowledge, support each other, and work towards common goals. Leaders can facilitate collaboration by organizing team-building activities, fostering cross-functional interactions, and creating opportunities for brainstorming and idea-sharing.

7. **Recognizing and Rewarding Achievement:** Celebrating individual and team achievements is crucial for maintaining motivation and building a positive team culture. A leader should recognize and reward exceptional performance, whether through public acknowledgment, incentives, or other forms of recognition. Recognizing achievements not only boosts morale but also encourages continuous improvement and a sense of pride in the team's work.

8. **Continuous Learning and Development:** High-performing teams

thrive on a culture of continuous learning and growth. A leader should provide opportunities for professional development, training, and skill enhancement. Encouraging team members to learn from their experiences, share knowledge, and stay updated with industry trends fosters a culture of innovation and adaptability within the team.

9. **Resolving Conflicts and Challenges:** Conflicts and challenges are inevitable within any team. A leader should proactively address conflicts, promote open dialogue, and mediate disputes to

ensure a healthy team dynamic. By fostering a culture of constructive feedback and resolving conflicts in a timely manner, a leader can prevent issues from escalating and maintain a positive work environment.

10. **Lead by Example:** Finally, leaders must lead by example. Team members look up to their leader for guidance and inspiration. Leaders should demonstrate the qualities they expect from their team members, such as professionalism, dedication, integrity, and a strong work ethic. By embodying the values and behaviors they promote,

leaders establish credibility and set the tone for the entire team.

Building a high-performing team is an ongoing process that requires consistent effort and adaptability. By implementing these principles, leaders can create an environment where individuals thrive, collaboration flourishes, and exceptional results are achieved.

9.3 Leading with Integrity

Leading with integrity is a fundamental principle of effective leadership that emphasizes honesty, ethical behavior, and moral principles. It involves leading by example and consistently demonstrating values such as honesty, trustworthiness, fairness, and accountability. When leaders prioritize integrity, they foster an environment of trust, loyalty, and respect, which ultimately leads to organizational success and personal growth.

Integrity begins with self-awareness and a deep understanding of one's values, beliefs, and ethical standards. Leaders who lead with integrity consistently align their actions and decisions with their core principles, even in the face of challenges or difficult choices. They act in a manner that is consistent with their values and do not compromise on their principles, even when it may be tempting or advantageous to do so.

Leading with integrity also requires transparency and open communication. Leaders who operate with integrity are honest and forthcoming with their team members, colleagues, and stakeholders. They share information openly, seek feedback, and encourage open dialogue. By promoting transparency, leaders create an environment where everyone feels valued, respected, and included, fostering a culture of trust and collaboration.

Furthermore, leading with integrity involves taking responsibility for one's actions and decisions. When mistakes are made, leaders with integrity acknowledge them, learn from them, and take appropriate measures to rectify the situation. They do not deflect blame or shift responsibility onto others. Instead, they demonstrate accountability and use failures as opportunities for growth and improvement.

Another aspect of leading with integrity is treating all individuals fairly and impartially. Leaders who uphold integrity do not play favorites or show bias. They make decisions based on merit and objective criteria, ensuring that everyone is given equal opportunities to succeed. Such leaders encourage diversity, inclusion, and a sense of belonging, valuing different perspectives and creating an inclusive environment where all individuals can thrive.

Leading with integrity also means adhering to ethical standards and legal requirements. Leaders who prioritize integrity do not engage in unethical or illegal practices, even if they believe it could benefit them or the organization in the short term. They understand the long-term consequences of such actions and make choices that are morally and ethically sound, even if they are challenging.

Additionally, leaders who lead with integrity build and maintain strong relationships based on trust and respect. They treat others with dignity, actively listen to their concerns, and value their input. They encourage collaboration, empower their team members, and recognize and appreciate their contributions. By fostering a culture of respect and trust, leaders create a supportive and productive work environment where individuals feel motivated and inspired to give their best.

In summary, leading with integrity is an essential leadership principle that encompasses honesty, ethical behavior, and moral principles. It involves aligning one's actions with their values, practicing transparency, taking responsibility, treating individuals fairly, adhering to ethical standards, and building strong relationships based on trust and respect. Leaders who prioritize integrity inspire trust, foster a positive work culture, and ultimately contribute to the long-term success and growth of their organization.

CHAPTER TEN

Mastering Negotiation Skills

10.1 Strategies for Win-Win Negotiations

Win-win negotiations aim to create mutually beneficial outcomes for all parties involved. These negotiations focus on collaboration, communication, and problem-solving to find solutions that satisfy the interests and needs of both sides. Here are some strategies for mastering win-win negotiations:

1. **Prepare and gather information:** Before entering a negotiation, it's essential to thoroughly research and understand the subject matter, the other party's interests, and potential areas of agreement or conflict. This knowledge will give you an advantage and help you propose creative solutions that meet both parties' needs.

2. **Focus on interests, not positions:** Instead of getting fixated on specific demands or positions, focus on understanding the underlying interests and motivations of both parties. By identifying common ground and shared

objectives, you can generate options that address these interests and create value for everyone involved.

3. **Build rapport and trust:** Establishing a positive and collaborative relationship with the other party is crucial for win-win negotiations. Actively listen to their perspective, acknowledge their concerns, and demonstrate empathy. Building trust will foster open communication and increase the likelihood of finding mutually beneficial solutions.

4. **Explore multiple options:** Encourage brainstorming and explore

various alternatives to find creative solutions. Look for integrative or "expanding the pie" options where both parties can gain value. Collaboratively generate and evaluate different ideas and be open to compromise.

5. **Communicate effectively:** Clear and effective communication is essential in win-win negotiations. Express your ideas and concerns clearly, using language that promotes understanding and cooperation. Be respectful and avoid confrontational or aggressive behavior. Active listening is equally important, as

it helps you understand the other party's needs and perspectives.

6. **Separate people from the problem:** Focus on addressing the problem or issue at hand rather than attacking the other party personally. Separate the people from the problem to maintain a constructive atmosphere. By collaborating to solve the problem together, you can work towards a win-win outcome.

7. **Emphasize long-term relationships:** Recognize that win-win negotiations are not just about the immediate outcome but also about

building long-term relationships. Prioritize maintaining a positive rapport and reputation, as it can lead to future opportunities for cooperation and mutual benefit.

8. **Develop a BATNA:** A Best Alternative to a Negotiated Agreement (BATNA) is the course of action you would pursue if the negotiation does not result in a satisfactory agreement. Having a well-defined BATNA strengthens your negotiation position and provides leverage. It allows you to negotiate from a position of strength and confidence

while also being open to finding mutually beneficial solutions.

9. **Seek objective criteria:** Whenever possible, use objective criteria, such as market value, industry standards, or expert opinions, to support your proposals. Relying on objective criteria helps depersonalize the negotiation and makes it easier to reach agreements that are fair and mutually beneficial.

10. **Be flexible and adaptable:** Negotiations often require flexibility and the ability to adapt to changing circumstances. Be open to adjusting your approach and exploring new

options as the negotiation unfolds. Maintaining a collaborative mindset and a willingness to find creative solutions will enhance your chances of reaching a win-win outcome.

Remember, mastering win-win negotiations is a skill that develops over time with practice and experience. By implementing these strategies and continuously refining your negotiation approach, you can become more effective at achieving mutually beneficial agreements.

10.2 Effective Persuasion Techniques

Effective persuasion techniques are vital in mastering negotiation skills. Persuasion involves the art of influencing others' thoughts, beliefs, and actions in order to achieve a desired outcome. When it comes to negotiations, being persuasive can help you sway opinions, build consensus, and ultimately reach mutually beneficial agreements. Here are some elaborations on effective persuasion techniques that can enhance your negotiation skills:

1. **Understand your audience:** Before engaging in a negotiation, it's crucial to thoroughly understand the individuals or groups you will be negotiating with.

This includes their interests, priorities, values, and any potential biases. By tailoring your persuasive tactics to resonate with their specific needs and motivations, you can increase the likelihood of a positive outcome.

2. **Build rapport and trust**: Persuasion is much more effective when there is a foundation of trust and rapport between the parties involved. Take the time to establish a connection with the other party, actively listen to their concerns, and show empathy towards their perspective. Building trust fosters open communication and increases the

chances of reaching a mutually beneficial agreement.

3. **Highlight shared interests:** Emphasize the common ground and shared interests between you and the other party. By framing the negotiation in a way that aligns with their goals and objectives, you can create a sense of collaboration rather than adversarial positions. This approach encourages both parties to work together towards finding win-win solutions.

4. **Present a compelling case:** Persuasion requires presenting a strong and logical argument to support your

position. Back your claims with relevant data, evidence, and examples to make your points more persuasive and credible. Anticipate potential counterarguments and address them proactively to strengthen your case.

5. **Use effective communication techniques:** Effective communication is a cornerstone of persuasion. Use clear and concise language, avoid jargon, and structure your arguments in a logical manner. Incorporate storytelling and vivid examples to make your message more engaging and relatable. Additionally, active listening and asking

thoughtful questions can help you understand the other party's perspective better and tailor your responses accordingly.

6. **Appeal to emotions:** While logical arguments are important, emotions play a significant role in decision-making. Appeal to the emotions of the other party by highlighting the potential benefits or positive outcomes that align with their values or aspirations. Use storytelling, vivid language, and imagery to evoke emotional responses that support your position.

7. **Offer incentives and concessions:** In negotiation, offering incentives or concessions can be a powerful persuasive technique. By demonstrating flexibility and willingness to compromise, you create an atmosphere of goodwill and reciprocity. Strategic concessions can also encourage the other party to reciprocate, leading to a more favorable outcome for both sides.

8. **Use social proof and authority:** Humans are influenced by the actions and opinions of others. Utilize social proof by presenting evidence of how your proposal or solution has been

successful in similar situations. Highlight testimonials, case studies, or endorsements from credible sources to bolster your credibility and persuade the other party to trust your proposal.

9. **Appeal to fairness and ethics:** Emphasize the fairness and ethical aspects of your proposal. Demonstrate how your solution provides equitable outcomes and aligns with commonly accepted ethical principles. By framing your argument in this manner, you can appeal to the other party's sense of justice and increase the likelihood of them accepting your proposal.

10. **Stay composed and adaptable:** Finally, maintaining composure and adaptability during negotiations is essential for effective persuasion. Be prepared to adjust your approach based on the dynamics of the negotiation. Remaining calm, composed, and respectful, even in challenging situations, can help you build credibility and increase the chances of a successful outcome.

Remember that effective persuasion techniques are not manipulative tactics aimed at solely benefiting one party. The goal is to create a collaborative environment where both parties feel heard and valued, leading to mutually beneficial agreements. By honing these skills, you can become a more persuasive negotiator and achieve positive outcomes in various negotiation scenarios.

10.3 Resolving Conflict and Reaching Agreements

Resolving conflicts and reaching agreements are crucial aspects of mastering negotiation skills. Negotiations often involve different parties with diverse interests and objectives, which can lead to conflicts and disagreements. Effective negotiators understand the importance of managing these conflicts and finding common ground to reach mutually beneficial agreements. In this response, we will discuss strategies and techniques for resolving conflicts and reaching agreements in the context of negotiations.

1. **Active Listening:** Active listening is a fundamental skill in negotiations. It involves giving full attention to the other party and seeking to understand their perspective, needs, and concerns. By actively listening, negotiators can uncover underlying issues and gain insights into potential areas of agreement. This helps in creating a more

collaborative atmosphere and demonstrating respect for the other party's views.

2. **Identify Interests:** During negotiations, it is essential to identify the underlying interests of each party involved. Interests are the needs, desires, concerns, and motivations that drive their positions. By understanding the interests of all parties, negotiators can find common ground and explore alternative solutions that satisfy those interests. Focusing on interests rather than rigid positions increases the

chances of reaching agreements that address everyone's concerns.

3. **Explore Multiple Options:** Effective negotiators consider multiple options and alternatives to resolve conflicts. They encourage brainstorming and creative thinking to generate a variety of potential solutions. By expanding the range of possibilities, negotiators can find innovative ways to meet the interests of all parties involved. This collaborative approach fosters a cooperative atmosphere and increases the likelihood of reaching mutually satisfactory agreements.

4. **Compromise and Trade-offs:** Negotiations often involve compromise and trade-offs. Skilled negotiators understand the importance of making concessions to reach agreements. They prioritize their objectives and identify areas where they can afford to give in to accommodate the interests of the other party. This willingness to make compromises helps build trust and encourages reciprocal concessions, leading to mutually beneficial outcomes.

5. **Win-Win Mindset:** Adopting a win-win mindset is crucial for successful negotiations. This approach emphasizes

seeking outcomes where all parties involved can benefit. Effective negotiators focus on creating value and maximizing mutual gains rather than engaging in adversarial tactics aimed at claiming a larger share of the pie. By seeking win-win solutions, negotiators build long-term relationships, enhance collaboration, and increase the chances of reaching sustainable agreements.

6. **Effective Communication:** Clear and effective communication is vital in resolving conflicts and reaching agreements. Negotiators should express their views, concerns, and proposals in a

concise and persuasive manner. They should also encourage open and honest communication from the other party. By fostering effective communication, negotiators can clarify misunderstandings, address concerns, and find common ground.

7. **Emotional Intelligence:** Emotional intelligence plays a significant role in negotiation. Skilled negotiators are aware of their emotions and manage them effectively during the negotiation process. They also recognize and respond to the emotions of the other party. By showing empathy and

understanding, negotiators can defuse tense situations, build rapport, and foster a cooperative environment that facilitates conflict resolution and agreement.

8. **Seek Mediation or Third-Party Assistance:** In some cases, resolving conflicts and reaching agreements may require the involvement of a neutral third party or mediator. Mediators can provide a fresh perspective, help manage emotions, and facilitate communication between the parties. They can assist in identifying common interests, exploring alternative solutions, and guiding the

negotiation process towards a mutually acceptable agreement.

In conclusion, mastering negotiation skills involves the ability to resolve conflicts and reach agreements. Effective negotiators employ active listening, identify interests, explore multiple options, and are willing to make compromises. They adopt a win-win mindset, communicate effectively, demonstrate emotional intelligence, and seek mediation when necessary. By employing these strategies and techniques, negotiators can navigate conflicts, find common ground, and achieve mutually beneficial agreements.

CHAPTER ELEVEN

Achieving Work-Life Balance

11.1 Prioritizing Personal Well-being

Prioritizing personal well-being is an essential aspect of achieving work-life balance. When we take care of ourselves physically, mentally, and emotionally, we are better equipped to handle the demands of work and personal life. Here are some elaborated strategies and practical examples to prioritize personal well-being:

a) **Establish Boundaries:** Set clear boundaries between work and personal life. Define specific times for work, family, relaxation, and self-care. Avoid bringing work-related tasks or stress into personal time. For instance, if you have a family dinner scheduled, make a conscious effort to disconnect from work by turning off notifications and focusing solely on spending quality time with your loved ones.

b) **Regular Exercise:** Engaging in regular physical exercise has numerous benefits for your well-being. It boosts energy levels, reduces stress, improves mood, and enhances overall health. Allocate time for physical activities that you enjoy, such as jogging, swimming, yoga, or playing a sport. For example, you could dedicate 30 minutes each morning for a brisk walk or schedule gym sessions during your lunch break.

c) **Take Breaks and Vacations:** Breaks are crucial for recharging and rejuvenating. Incorporate short breaks throughout the workday to relax and clear your mind. Avoid skipping lunch or working excessively long hours without rest. Additionally, plan and take regular vacations to completely disconnect from work and focus on personal enjoyment and relaxation. During vacations, immerse yourself in activities that bring you joy, whether it's traveling, reading, or pursuing a hobby.

d) **Practice Mindfulness and Stress Reduction Techniques:** Mindfulness and stress reduction techniques can help manage work-related stress and promote well-being. Allocate time each day for mindfulness practices such as meditation, deep breathing exercises, or journaling. These practices can help calm your mind, reduce anxiety, and improve focus. For instance, you could incorporate a 10-minute meditation session in the morning or practice deep breathing exercises during stressful work moments.

e) **Prioritize Sleep:** Sufficient sleep is vital for overall well-being and productivity. Establish a consistent sleep schedule and ensure you get the recommended 7-9 hours of quality sleep each night. Create a bedtime routine that promotes relaxation, such as reading a book, listening to soothing music, or taking a warm bath. Avoid bringing work-related devices into the bedroom to minimize distractions and enhance sleep quality.

f) **Nourish Your Body:** Pay attention to your nutritional intake and make healthy food choices. Incorporate a balanced diet with fruits, vegetables, whole grains, and lean proteins. Stay hydrated by drinking an adequate amount of water throughout the day. Avoid relying on processed foods or excessive caffeine intake, as they can negatively impact your energy levels and overall well-being.

g) **Foster Supportive Relationships:**

Nurture relationships with family,

friends, and loved ones. Make time for social activities and maintain meaningful connections. Engage in activities that bring you joy and enable you to bond with others. For example, plan regular outings with friends or organize family game nights to strengthen relationships and create lasting memories.

h) **Pursue Personal Interests and Hobbies:** Dedicate time to activities you genuinely enjoy and that bring you a sense of fulfillment outside of work. Whether it's painting, playing a musical instrument, gardening, or practicing a sport, allocate time each week for your hobbies. Engaging in activities you love helps reduce stress, boost creativity, and bring balance to your life.

Remember, prioritizing personal well-being is an ongoing process that requires self-awareness and commitment. By incorporating these strategies and examples into your daily routine, you can foster a healthier work-life balance and enhance your overall quality of life.

11.2 Managing Stress and Burnout

Managing stress and burnout is crucial for achieving a healthy work-life balance. When individuals become overwhelmed by excessive job demands and face prolonged periods of stress, it can lead to burnout—a state of physical, emotional, and mental exhaustion. By adopting effective strategies to manage stress and prevent burnout, individuals can maintain their well-being and enhance their overall quality of life. Here are some practical examples of managing stress and burnout:

a) **Setting Boundaries:** Establish clear boundaries between work and personal life. This involves defining specific working hours and sticking to them. Avoid bringing work-related tasks into personal time, such as checking emails or taking work calls during family or leisure activities.

Example: If you work from home, create a dedicated workspace and treat it as a separate area solely for work. When you finish work for the day, leave the workspace and mentally switch off from work-related matters.

b) **Prioritizing Self-Care:** Engage in activities that promote self-care and relaxation. This can include exercise, hobbies, meditation, spending time with loved ones, or pursuing personal interests. Taking care of oneself physically and mentally helps recharge energy levels and reduce stress.

Example: Dedicate at least 30 minutes each day to engage in an activity you enjoy, such as going for a walk, practicing yoga, reading a book, or listening to music. This designated time for self-care can act as a buffer against work-related stress.

> c) **Time Management:** Efficiently manage time to avoid becoming overwhelmed by work tasks. Prioritize tasks based on their urgency and importance, and break them down into manageable chunks. Avoid overcommitting and learn to say no when necessary.

Example: Use productivity tools or techniques like the Pomodoro Technique, where you work for a focused 25 minutes followed by a short break. This approach can help maintain concentration and prevent burnout from long periods of uninterrupted work.

    d) **Support Network:** Build a strong support network of friends, family, and colleagues. Seek support from them when feeling overwhelmed or stressed. Discussing challenges and sharing experiences with others can provide valuable perspective and emotional support.

Example: Join professional networks or online communities related to your field, where you can connect with like-minded individuals facing similar challenges. Engaging in discussions and seeking advice can alleviate feelings of isolation and provide valuable insights.

- e) **Vacation and Time Off:** Take regular breaks, including vacations and days off. Disconnecting from work for a period allows for relaxation, rejuvenation, and the opportunity to recharge both physically and mentally.

Example: Plan vacations or staycations where you disconnect from work completely. Use pg. 230

auto-responders to set clear expectations about your unavailability during that time and delegate responsibilities to colleagues if necessary.

    f) **Seek Professional Help:** If stress and burnout persist despite self-help strategies, consider seeking professional help from therapists, counselors, or coaches. These professionals can provide guidance, support, and coping strategies tailored to individual needs.

Example: If you notice persistent signs of burnout, such as chronic fatigue, decreased motivation, or difficulty concentrating, consult with a mental health professional who can help identify underlying causes and develop a personalized plan for recovery.

Remember, managing stress and preventing burnout is an ongoing process that requires self-awareness and regular evaluation. By implementing these strategies and making self-care a priority, individuals can effectively manage stress, avoid burnout, and achieve a healthy work-life balance.

11.3 Creating Harmony between Work and Life

Achieving work-life balance is a crucial aspect of maintaining overall well-being and happiness in today's fast-paced and demanding world. It involves finding a harmonious integration between professional commitments and personal life, allowing individuals to fulfill their responsibilities at work while also enjoying their personal interests, relationships, and leisure time. Here, I will elaborate on practical examples and strategies for creating harmony between work and life.

a) **Establish clear boundaries:** Setting clear boundaries between work and personal life is essential. Define specific work hours and commit to sticking to them as much as possible. Avoid bringing work-related tasks or stress into personal time and vice versa. For example, you can turn off work-related notifications on your phone during evenings and weekends to focus on personal activities or spend quality time with loved ones.

b) **Prioritize and delegate tasks:** Efficiently managing your workload is key to achieving work-life balance. Prioritize your tasks based on their importance and deadlines. Delegate responsibilities whenever possible, ensuring that the workload is evenly distributed. This approach allows you to avoid excessive stress and frees up time for personal pursuits. For instance, if you're a team leader, delegate tasks to team members based on their skills and strengths, enabling you to focus on higher-level responsibilities.

c) **Practice effective time management:** Utilize time management techniques to optimize productivity and create more time for personal activities. Prioritize your work tasks based on their urgency and importance. Break large tasks into smaller, manageable chunks to avoid feeling overwhelmed. Additionally, consider using productivity tools, such as calendars, to schedule and track your activities effectively. By efficiently managing your time, you can allocate dedicated periods for personal activities like hobbies, exercise, or spending time with family and friends.

d) **Learn to say no:** It's essential to set boundaries by learning to say no when necessary. Taking on too many commitments can lead to burnout and neglect of personal life. Assess the demands on your time and energy before committing to additional tasks or projects. It's important to remember that saying no to certain things allows you to say yes to others, such as personal goals or quality time with loved ones.

e) **Foster a supportive work environment:** Encourage a workplace culture that values work-life balance and supports employees' well-being. This includes flexible working hours, remote work options, and policies that promote a healthy work-life integration. Organizations can introduce initiatives like wellness programs, stress management workshops, and employee assistance programs to help employees cope with work-related stressors and create a conducive work environment.

f) **Unplug and recharge:** Taking regular breaks from work and technology is essential for recharging and rejuvenating. Make it a habit to disconnect from work-related devices and activities during breaks or vacations. Engage in activities that help you relax and recharge, such as meditation, exercise, hobbies, or spending time in nature. By allowing yourself dedicated time away from work, you can return with renewed focus and energy.

g) **Communicate and involve loved ones:** Open communication with family members, friends, and colleagues is crucial. Discuss your work commitments, goals, and challenges with loved ones, seeking their understanding and support. Involve them in decision-making processes and find ways to share responsibilities, ensuring that everyone's needs are taken into consideration. This approach promotes mutual support and understanding, strengthening personal relationships.

For example, let's say you have a work presentation scheduled on a day when you had planned to attend your child's school event. By communicating your situation to your supervisor and proposing an alternative solution, such as rescheduling the presentation or delegating the task, you can find a compromise that allows you to attend the school event without compromising your professional commitments.

Remember, achieving work-life balance is an ongoing process that requires regular evaluation, adjustment, and self-care. By implementing these strategies and finding what works best for you, you can create harmony between work and life, leading to improved well-being and overall satisfaction.

CHAPTER TWELVE

Leveraging Technology for Success

12.1 Embracing Digital Transformation

Embracing digital transformation has become crucial for businesses and organizations across industries to stay competitive and achieve success in today's rapidly evolving digital landscape. The phrase "leverage technology for success" perfectly encapsulates the essence of digital transformation, which involves adopting and integrating digital technologies and processes into various aspects of business operations to drive growth, enhance customer experiences, and streamline internal processes. In this response, I will elaborate on the concept of embracing digital transformation, providing practical examples to illustrate its significance and potential benefits.

Enhanced Customer Experiences:

Digital transformation empowers businesses to deliver personalized and seamless customer experiences. For instance, e-commerce platforms leverage data analytics and AI algorithms to recommend products based on customer preferences, browsing history, and purchase behavior. Additionally, companies can leverage chatbots and virtual assistants to provide 24/7 customer support, resolving queries and addressing concerns promptly. By embracing digital technologies, businesses can create tailored experiences that cater to individual customer needs and preferences.

Example: Amazon, the world's largest online retailer, leverages digital transformation to provide a personalized shopping experience. They use advanced algorithms to suggest products, offer personalized recommendations, and facilitate easy purchasing with features like one-click ordering and same-day delivery.

Streamlined Operations:

Digital transformation enables businesses to optimize and automate their internal processes, improving efficiency, and reducing costs. Cloud computing, for instance, allows organizations to store and access data remotely, eliminating the need for physical servers and reducing maintenance overhead. Furthermore, automation tools and robotic process automation (RPA) can streamline repetitive tasks, such as data entry and invoice processing, freeing up valuable time for employees to focus on more strategic and value-added activities.

Example: Tesla, the electric vehicle manufacturer, embraces digital transformation by leveraging automation and robotics in their production processes. They use robots to assemble components, reducing manual labor and increasing production efficiency. Additionally, they have implemented digital tools and software to streamline supply chain management, enabling real-time tracking of inventory and optimizing logistics operations.

Data-driven Decision Making:

Digital transformation empowers businesses to make data-driven decisions by harnessing the power of analytics and business intelligence tools. By collecting and analyzing large volumes of data, organizations can gain valuable insights into customer behavior, market trends, and operational performance. These insights enable businesses to make informed decisions, identify areas for improvement, and uncover new opportunities for growth.

Example: Netflix, the popular streaming service, relies on digital transformation to drive its content strategy. They collect and analyze vast amounts of user data, including viewing preferences, search history, and ratings, to recommend personalized content to their subscribers. This data-driven approach allows Netflix to continuously optimize their content library, ensuring that users have a tailored and engaging viewing experience.

Agile and Innovative Culture:

Embracing digital transformation fosters an agile and innovative culture within organizations. By embracing new technologies and processes, businesses can adapt quickly to changing market conditions and customer demands. This agility enables organizations to stay ahead of competitors and seize new opportunities. Moreover, digital transformation encourages a culture of innovation, where employees are empowered to experiment, test new ideas, and embrace change.

Example: Google, the multinational technology company, promotes a culture of innovation and digital transformation. They encourage their employees to spend 20% of their time on passion projects, which has led to the development of innovative products such as Gmail and Google Maps. This approach allows Google to continually explore new ideas and stay at the forefront of technological advancements.

In conclusion, embracing digital transformation is essential for businesses and organizations to thrive in today's digital age.

By leveraging technology, organizations can enhance customer experiences, streamline operations, make data-driven decisions, and foster an agile and innovative culture. The examples provided demonstrate how prominent companies have successfully embraced digital transformation to achieve success and maintain a competitive edge in their respective industries.

12.2 Tools and Technologies for Efficiency

Leveraging technology for success is an essential strategy in today's fast-paced and competitive business landscape. With the right tools and technologies, organizations can improve their efficiency, productivity, and overall performance. In this response, I will elaborate on various tools and technologies that can be employed to enhance efficiency in different aspects of business operations, along with practical examples.

Project Management Tools:

Efficient project management is crucial for successful execution and timely delivery of tasks. Project management tools like Trello, Asana, or Monday.com enable teams to collaborate, assign tasks, set deadlines, and track progress in real-time. These tools provide a visual representation of the project workflow, making it easier to identify bottlenecks, allocate resources efficiently, and ensure that everyone is on the same page.

Example: A marketing team can use Trello to manage their content creation process. They can create boards for different projects, assign tasks to team members, set due dates, and monitor the progress of each content piece. This enables the team to streamline their workflow, identify any delays, and ensure that content is delivered on time.

Communication and Collaboration Tools:

Efficient communication and collaboration are vital for seamless teamwork, especially in distributed or remote work environments. Tools like Slack, Microsoft Teams, or Google Workspace provide instant messaging, video conferencing, file sharing, and collaborative document editing features. These tools facilitate effective communication, quick decision-making, and knowledge sharing among team members.

Example: A software development team can utilize Slack for real-time communication. They can create channels for different projects, discuss technical issues, share code snippets, and receive instant feedback. This reduces the need for lengthy email threads, allows for quicker problem-solving, and enhances overall team productivity.

Customer Relationship Management (CRM) Systems:

CRM systems are designed to manage and streamline customer interactions, sales processes, and customer data. These tools, such as Salesforce, HubSpot, or Zoho CRM, centralize customer information, automate sales workflows, track customer interactions, and provide valuable insights for better customer engagement. By utilizing CRM systems, businesses can enhance their efficiency in sales and customer service activities.

Example: A sales team can utilize Salesforce to manage their customer relationships. They can store customer information, track interactions, schedule follow-ups, and automate repetitive tasks like email outreach. By having a centralized system, sales reps can quickly access customer data, streamline their sales pipeline, and provide personalized experiences to prospects and customers.

Automation and Workflow Tools:

Automation tools allow businesses to automate repetitive and time-consuming tasks, reducing manual effort and minimizing errors. Tools like Zapier, IFTTT, or Microsoft Power Automate enable seamless integration between different apps and services, allowing for the automation of workflows and data transfer across platforms.

Example: A marketing team can leverage Zapier to automate their lead generation process. They can set up triggers to capture leads from various sources (e.g., website forms, social media ads) and automatically add them to the CRM system. This eliminates the need for manual data entry, saves time, and ensures that no leads are missed.

Data Analytics and Business Intelligence Tools:

Data analytics and business intelligence tools help organizations make informed decisions by analyzing and visualizing data. Tools like Tableau, Google Analytics, or Microsoft Power BI provide insights into business performance, customer behavior, and market trends. By leveraging these tools, businesses can identify patterns, spot opportunities, and optimize their operations for increased efficiency.

Example: An e-commerce company can use Google Analytics to analyze website traffic and customer behavior. They can track metrics like conversion rates, bounce rates, and average session duration to identify areas for improvement. With this information, they can optimize their website design, streamline the purchasing process, and enhance overall user experience.

In conclusion, by leveraging various tools and technologies, organizations can significantly improve their efficiency across different areas of business operations. Whether it's project management, communication, customer relationship management, automation, or data analytics, the right tools empower businesses to streamline workflows, enhance collaboration, and make data-driven decisions, ultimately leading to success in today's competitive landscape.

12.3 Navigating the Digital Landscape

In today's fast-paced and ever-evolving world, leveraging technology for success has become the bedrock of any business or individual's growth strategy. One of the key aspects of this strategy is navigating the digital landscape effectively. The digital landscape encompasses various online platforms, tools, and technologies that can be harnessed to drive growth, enhance productivity, and achieve success. In this elaboration, I will delve into the concept of navigating the digital landscape, providing practical examples to illustrate its significance and how it can be achieved.

Online Presence and Branding:

Establishing a strong online presence is crucial for businesses and individuals alike. It involves creating and maintaining a consistent brand image across various digital channels. By leveraging technology, businesses can develop visually appealing websites, optimize their content for search engines, and engage with their target audience through social media platforms. For instance, a small business owner can utilize social media marketing tools such as Facebook Ads or Instagram influencers to promote their products or services, expanding their reach and driving sales.

E-commerce and Digital Marketplaces:

The rise of e-commerce has revolutionized the way businesses operate and consumers shop. Navigating the digital landscape involves embracing online marketplaces such as Amazon, eBay, or Alibaba, as well as building and optimizing one's own e-commerce platform. These platforms enable businesses to reach a wider customer base, offer personalized shopping experiences, and streamline the purchasing process. A practical example would be a local artisan who establishes an online store on Etsy, showcasing their handmade products to a global audience, and benefiting from the convenience and accessibility of online transactions.

Data Analytics and Insights:

Data is a powerful asset in the digital landscape. With the help of technology, businesses can collect, analyze, and derive actionable insights from large volumes of data. This information can be used to make informed decisions, optimize operations, and identify emerging trends or customer preferences. For example, an e-commerce retailer can use data analytics tools to track customer behavior, identify popular products, and personalize recommendations, leading to increased customer satisfaction and sales.

Automation and Artificial Intelligence (AI):

Automation and AI technologies play a significant role in navigating the digital landscape. These technologies can streamline repetitive tasks, improve efficiency, and enhance customer experiences. Chatbots, for instance, can provide instant customer support, answer frequently asked questions, and assist with basic transactions, freeing up human resources for more complex tasks. Automation can also be applied to email marketing campaigns, content distribution, inventory management, and other business processes, saving time and resources while increasing productivity.

Collaboration and Communication:

Technology facilitates seamless collaboration and communication, regardless of geographical boundaries. Cloud-based tools such as project management software, file-sharing platforms, and video conferencing solutions enable teams to collaborate in real-time, share information, and work together effectively. For instance, a multinational company can leverage video conferencing tools like Zoom or Microsoft Teams to conduct virtual meetings, bringing together employees from different locations, reducing travel costs, and improving communication and decision-making.

Cybersecurity and Data Privacy:

Navigating the digital landscape also requires a focus on cybersecurity and data privacy. As businesses and individuals become more reliant on technology, protecting sensitive information and guarding against cyber threats is paramount. Implementing robust security measures, employing encryption techniques, and staying updated with the latest security protocols are essential steps in maintaining a secure digital presence. For example, an online banking institution must invest in advanced security systems to safeguard customer data and financial transactions, building trust and confidence among its users.

In conclusion, navigating the digital landscape is a fundamental aspect of leveraging technology for success. By establishing a strong online presence, embracing e-commerce platforms, harnessing the power of data analytics and AI, facilitating collaboration and communication, and prioritizing cybersecurity, businesses and individuals can seize the opportunities presented by the digital age. The practical examples provided demonstrate how technology can be effectively utilized to drive growth, enhance productivity, and ultimately achieve success in the digital landscape.

CHAPTER THIRTEEN

Financial Strategies for Success

13.1 Building Wealth and Financial Independence

Building wealth and achieving financial independence are important goals for many individuals. They require careful planning, disciplined saving and investing, and a long-term perspective. "Financial Strategies for Success" can serve as a bedrock for achieving these goals by providing a framework and guiding principles to follow. Let's delve into some practical examples of how to build wealth and attain financial independence.

Create a Budget and Track Expenses:

One of the fundamental steps towards building wealth is creating a budget. Start by analyzing your income and expenses to understand where your money is going. Categorize your expenses into essential (such as housing, transportation, and groceries) and discretionary (entertainment, dining out, vacations). Look for opportunities to reduce unnecessary expenses and redirect those funds towards savings and investments. Regularly tracking your expenses helps you stay accountable and make informed financial decisions.

Example: Let's say you analyze your expenses and find that you're spending a significant portion of your income on dining out. By reducing your restaurant visits and preparing meals at home, you can save hundreds of dollars each month. Redirecting those savings towards investments can accelerate your wealth-building journey.

Save and Invest:

Saving and investing are critical components of wealth-building. Set aside a portion of your income each month and make it a habit to save consistently. Aim to build an emergency fund that covers at least three to six months' worth of living expenses. Once you have an adequate emergency fund, start investing to grow your wealth over time. Consider a diversified portfolio of stocks, bonds, mutual funds, or exchange-traded funds (ETFs) that align with your risk tolerance and financial goals.

Example: Let's assume you allocate 20% of your monthly income towards savings and investments. Over time, this disciplined approach will allow your investments to compound, generating returns and growing your wealth. As your investments grow, they can generate additional income, such as dividends or capital gains, further accelerating your path to financial independence.

Minimize Debt and Manage Credit:

Debt can hinder wealth-building efforts, so it's essential to minimize high-interest debt and manage credit wisely. Pay off credit card balances in full each month to avoid interest charges. Prioritize paying off high-interest debts, such as credit card debt or personal loans. Additionally, consider refinancing loans to secure lower interest rates and reduce monthly payments. By managing debt effectively, you can free up more funds for savings and investments.

Example: Let's say you have a high-interest credit card debt of $5,000 with an interest rate of 18%. By aggressively paying down this debt, you can save hundreds or even thousands of dollars in interest charges. Once the debt is cleared, redirect the money that was previously allocated towards debt payments into your savings and investment accounts.

Diversify Income Sources:

Relying solely on a single source of income can limit your wealth-building potential. Consider diversifying your income sources to create additional streams of revenue. This can be achieved through various means, such as starting a side business, investing in rental properties, or generating passive income through dividend-paying stocks or real estate investment trusts (REITs). Diversifying your income sources not only increases your earning potential but also provides a safety net against potential job loss or economic downturns.

Example: Let's imagine you have a full-time job but also start a small online business. By dedicating a few hours a week to your side business, you can generate additional income that can be used for savings and investments. Over time, if your business grows, it can become a significant contributor to your wealth-building efforts.

Continuously Educate Yourself:

Financial literacy is crucial for making informed decisions and optimizing your wealth-building strategy. Continuously educate yourself about personal finance, investing, and wealth management. Read books, follow reputable financial blogs and websites, attend seminars or workshops, and engage in discussions with financial professionals. By staying informed and up-to-date on financial matters, you can make sound financial decisions and adapt your strategies as needed.

For example, let's say you have some extra savings and are considering different investment options. Through continuous education, you may come across a book that explains the benefits of diversifying your investment portfolio. By understanding the concept of diversification and learning about various investment vehicles such as stocks, bonds, real estate, and mutual funds, you can make an informed decision on how to allocate your funds. This knowledge can help you mitigate risk and potentially earn higher returns over the long term.

Another practical example of continuous education is staying updated on tax laws and regulations. Tax rules are subject to change, and being aware of any new legislation or amendments can help you optimize your tax strategy. By understanding the available deductions, credits, and tax-efficient investment vehicles, you can minimize your tax liability and keep more money working for you.

Moreover, continuous education can enhance your financial discipline and decision-making abilities. As you educate yourself, you gain a better understanding of the factors that influence financial markets, economic trends, and personal financial planning. This knowledge allows you to make informed decisions based on a solid foundation, rather than relying on impulsive or uninformed choices.

It's important to note that continuous education doesn't necessarily mean formal education or expensive courses. There are numerous free or low-cost resources available to expand your financial knowledge. Here are a few examples:

Books: There are countless personal finance and investment books available that cover a wide range of topics. Some popular titles include "The Intelligent Investor" by Benjamin Graham, "Rich Dad Poor Dad" by Robert Kiyosaki, and "A Random Walk Down Wall Street" by Burton Malkiel.

I. **Online Resources:** Reputable financial websites, blogs, and forums provide valuable information on personal finance, investing strategies, and wealth management. Websites like Investopedia, The Balance, and

NerdWallet offer comprehensive guides, articles, and tools to help you understand various financial concepts.

II. **Podcasts:** Financial podcasts have gained popularity in recent years, offering insights and advice from experts in the field. Podcasts like "The Dave Ramsey Show," "The Mad Fientist Financial Independence Podcast," and "ChooseFI" cover a range of topics related to building wealth and achieving financial independence.

III. **Webinars and Seminars:** Many financial institutions, investment firms, and community organizations host webinars and seminars on personal finance and investment topics. These events often feature industry experts who share valuable insights and strategies.

Remember, building wealth and achieving financial independence is a lifelong journey. By continuously educating yourself, you equip yourself with the knowledge and tools needed to make informed decisions, adapt to changing circumstances, and optimize your financial strategies.

13.2 Effective Budgeting and Saving

Building wealth and achieving financial independence are significant goals for many individuals. To accomplish these objectives, it is crucial to develop effective financial strategies that provide a solid foundation for success. In this response, we will explore various strategies and provide practical examples to help you build wealth and attain financial independence.

  I. **Create a Budget:** One of the fundamental steps in building wealth is to establish a budget. A budget allows you to track your income and expenses, helping you allocate your resources effectively. By understanding where your money is going, you can identify areas where you can cut back on unnecessary spending and redirect those funds towards wealth-building activities. For instance, you might discover that you're spending a significant amount on dining out. By reducing your dining out expenses and cooking at home more often, you can save money and invest it in assets that generate long-term returns.

II. **Save and Invest:** Saving and investing are critical components of building wealth. Start by building an emergency fund that covers three to six months' worth of living expenses. This provides a safety net for unexpected financial challenges. Once you have an emergency fund in place, focus on investing your savings in various asset classes such as stocks, bonds, real estate, or mutual funds. Let's say you have $10,000 to invest. By investing this amount in a diversified portfolio with a balanced mix of stocks and bonds, you can potentially earn higher returns over time compared to leaving the money idle in a savings account.

III. **Take Advantage of Retirement Accounts:** Retirement accounts, such as 401(k)s or Individual Retirement Accounts (IRAs), offer tax advantages and are powerful tools for building long-term wealth. These accounts provide tax benefits on contributions and allow your investments to grow tax-deferred or tax-free. For example, if your employer offers a 401(k) matching program, contribute enough to maximize the matching funds. This is essentially free money that boosts your retirement savings and accelerates your wealth-building journey.

IV. **Diversify Your Income Streams:** Relying solely on a single source of income can be risky. To build wealth and achieve financial independence, consider diversifying your income streams. This can involve starting a side business, investing in rental properties, or generating passive income through investments in dividend-paying stocks or peer-to-peer lending platforms. By diversifying your income, you create multiple streams of cash flow that can support your wealth-building efforts and provide stability in uncertain economic times.

V. **Minimize Debt and Manage Credit Wisely:** High levels of debt can hinder your ability to build wealth and achieve financial independence. Minimize consumer debt, such as credit card debt, by paying off balances in full each month and avoiding unnecessary purchases. Prioritize paying off high-interest debts like student loans or personal loans. By reducing your debt burden, you free up cash flow that can be redirected towards wealth-building activities.

VI. **Continuously Educate Yourself:** Financial literacy is a crucial aspect of building wealth. Educate yourself on personal finance topics, investment strategies, and wealth-building techniques. Read books, attend seminars, or take online courses to enhance your knowledge. For instance, learning about real estate investing can provide insights into acquiring properties that generate rental income and appreciate in value over time.

VII. **Practice Long-Term Thinking:** Building wealth is a marathon, not a sprint. Practice patience and discipline by focusing on long-term goals rather than short-term gains. Avoid chasing speculative investments or get-rich-quick schemes that promise overnight success. Instead, develop a long-term investment plan aligned with your financial goals and risk tolerance. For example, investing in a well-diversified stock portfolio and holding it for the long haul can lead to significant wealth accumulation over several decades.

VIII. **Seek Professional Advice:** Consider working with a financial advisor who can provide personalized guidance based on your financial situation and goals. A financial advisor can help you develop a comprehensive financial plan, provide investment advice, and keep you accountable to your wealth-building strategies. They can also assist in optimizing your tax strategies and help navigate complex financial decisions.

In conclusion, building wealth and achieving financial independence requires a combination of sound financial strategies and disciplined execution. By creating a budget, saving and investing wisely, diversifying income streams, minimizing debt, continuously educating yourself, practicing long-term thinking, and seeking professional advice, you can establish a solid foundation for long-term financial success. Remember, building wealth takes time and consistent effort, but with the right strategies and mindset, you can achieve your financial goals.

13.3 Investing for Long-Term Success

Investing for long-term success is a crucial component of a sound financial strategy. It involves making strategic investment decisions with a focus on the long run, aiming to achieve growth, build wealth, and secure financial stability over an extended period of time. By adopting a long-term perspective, investors can benefit from compounding returns, ride out market fluctuations, and take advantage of opportunities for substantial gains. In this response, I will elaborate on the concept of investing for long-term success and provide practical examples to illustrate its effectiveness.

Start Early and Harness the Power of Compounding:

One of the most powerful advantages of long-term investing is the ability to leverage compounding returns. Compounding occurs when your investment gains generate additional returns over time. By starting to invest early, you allow your investments to grow and accumulate wealth steadily. Let's take an example to illustrate this. Suppose you invest $1,000 annually in a retirement account from the age of 25 to 35 and then stop contributing. Assuming an average annual return of 8%, by the time you reach 65, your investment will have grown to approximately $198,000. However, if you start investing at 35 and continue until 65 with the same annual contribution, you would only have around $168,000. Starting early gives your investments more time to compound, resulting in a substantial difference in the final portfolio value.

Diversify Your Portfolio:

Diversification is a crucial aspect of long-term investing. It involves spreading your investments across different asset classes, sectors, and geographic regions to reduce risk. By diversifying, you mitigate the impact of any single investment performing poorly. For instance, instead of investing all your money in a single stock, you can allocate a portion to stocks, bonds, real estate, and other asset classes. This strategy helps protect your portfolio against market downturns and provides potential upside from various sources. By diversifying, you can take advantage of different investment opportunities while reducing the risk of significant losses.

Embrace a Buy-and-Hold Approach:

Long-term success in investing often stems from adopting a buy-and-hold strategy rather than trying to time the market. Timing the market involves making investment decisions based on short-term price fluctuations, which is notoriously difficult and often results in poor performance. On the other hand, a buy-and-hold approach involves investing in fundamentally strong companies or assets and holding them for an extended period, irrespective of short-term market volatility. This strategy allows you to benefit from the long-term growth potential of quality investments. Consider the example of Warren

Buffett, one of the most successful investors of all time. Buffett's investment philosophy revolves around finding undervalued companies with strong fundamentals and holding them for the long haul. By adhering to this approach, Buffett has generated substantial wealth over decades.

Reinvest Dividends:

Another effective strategy for long-term investing is reinvesting dividends. Dividends are payments made by companies to their shareholders as a share of the company's profits. Instead of taking the dividend payments in cash, you can choose to reinvest them back into the same company or other investments. By reinvesting dividends, you can harness the power of compounding mentioned earlier.

Let's consider an example to understand the impact of reinvesting dividends. Suppose you invest $10,000 in a dividend-paying stock that has an average annual dividend yield of 4%. If you choose to reinvest the dividends over a 20-year period, assuming a consistent dividend yield and no change in the stock's price, your investment would grow to approximately $21,911. However, if you opt to take the dividends in cash, your investment would only be worth $14,800. Reinvesting dividends allows you to accumulate more shares over time, increasing your potential for future returns.

Rebalance Your Portfolio Periodically:

To ensure your investment portfolio remains aligned with your long-term goals and risk tolerance, it is important to periodically rebalance your portfolio. Rebalancing involves reviewing your investments and making adjustments to maintain the desired asset allocation. Over time, some investments may outperform others, causing the allocation to deviate from your original plan. By rebalancing, you sell a portion of the investments that have performed well and reinvest the proceeds into underperforming assets. This disciplined approach helps to control risk and maintain a balanced portfolio.

For example, suppose you initially set a target allocation of 60% stocks and 40% bonds. After a few years, due to strong stock market performance, the stock portion of your portfolio has increased to 70%. To rebalance, you would sell some of your stocks and reallocate the funds to bonds to bring your portfolio back to the desired 60/40 allocation. This strategy ensures that your portfolio remains diversified and reduces the potential negative impact of any single asset class.

Stay Informed and Seek Professional Advice:

Investing for long-term success requires ongoing education and staying informed about the financial markets and investment opportunities. While there is a wealth of information available, it is crucial to critically evaluate the sources and seek professional advice when needed. Financial advisors can provide guidance tailored to your specific circumstances and help you navigate through different market conditions.

In conclusion, investing for long-term success involves adopting a strategic approach that leverages the power of compounding, diversification, a buy-and-hold strategy, reinvesting dividends, periodic rebalancing, and staying informed. By implementing these practices, you increase your chances of achieving growth, building wealth, and securing financial stability over an extended period of time. Remember, investing involves risk, and it's important to assess your own risk tolerance and consult with professionals before making any investment decisions.

CHAPTER FOURTEEN

Continuous Learning and Growth

14.1 The Value of Lifelong Learning

The value of lifelong learning cannot be overstated in today's rapidly evolving world. In a society driven by innovation and technological advancements, the ability to continuously learn and grow is essential for personal and professional success. Lifelong learning goes beyond formal education and encompasses the pursuit of knowledge and skills throughout one's life, regardless of age or stage of career. It serves as a catalyst for personal development, career advancement, adaptability, and overall fulfillment.

One of the primary benefits of lifelong learning is personal development. Engaging in learning activities broadens our horizons, deepens our understanding of the world, and enhances our critical thinking skills. It enables us to explore new interests, discover hidden talents, and develop a well-rounded perspective. For example, an individual who has a passion for art may take up painting classes later in life. Through this learning experience, they not only acquire new artistic skills but also gain a greater appreciation for different forms of art and culture, fostering personal growth and self-expression.

Lifelong learning is also crucial for career advancement. In today's competitive job market, skills become outdated at an alarming rate. Continuous learning allows individuals to stay relevant and adapt to changing industry demands. For instance, professionals in the field of technology must constantly update their knowledge and learn new programming languages or tools to remain competitive. By investing time and effort into lifelong learning, individuals enhance their professional skill sets, improve their job prospects, and increase their earning potential.

Furthermore, lifelong learning promotes adaptability and resilience. The ability to learn and adapt to new situations and challenges is a valuable asset in an ever-changing world. For example, consider an employee who has been working in a specific industry for many years. If technological advancements disrupt the industry or the company undergoes a significant organizational change, those who have embraced lifelong learning will be better equipped to adapt to the new circumstances. They can quickly acquire new skills, understand emerging trends, and navigate through uncertainty with ease, ultimately ensuring their professional relevance and employability.

Lifelong learning also contributes to personal fulfillment and well-being. Engaging in intellectually stimulating activities and continuously expanding one's knowledge not only keeps the mind active but also provides a sense of purpose and satisfaction. Learning new things can bring joy, boost self-confidence, and increase overall life satisfaction. For instance, an individual who takes up a hobby such as learning a musical instrument experiences a sense of accomplishment as they progress in their skills, leading to a greater sense of fulfillment and happiness.

Moreover, lifelong learning fosters curiosity, creativity, and innovation. When we expose ourselves to new ideas, concepts, and perspectives, it sparks our curiosity and fuels our imagination. By connecting seemingly unrelated pieces of knowledge, we can generate innovative solutions to problems and make significant contributions in various fields. The famous physicist Albert Einstein once said, "I have no special talent. I am only passionately curious." This statement highlights the importance of continuous learning and curiosity in driving breakthrough discoveries and advancements.

In conclusion, lifelong learning is of immense value in today's fast-paced and dynamic world. It enables personal development, promotes career advancement, enhances adaptability, and contributes to overall fulfillment. By embracing the mindset of continuous learning and growth, individuals can stay ahead of the curve, seize new opportunities, and navigate through the complexities of modern life with confidence. Lifelong learning is not only a bedrock for personal success but also a means to contribute positively to society and make a lasting impact.

14.2 Seeking Personal and Professional Development

Seeking personal and professional development is a crucial aspect of continuous learning and growth. It involves actively pursuing opportunities for self-improvement, acquiring new skills, expanding knowledge, and enhancing one's abilities to excel both personally and in the professional realm. This mindset is driven by the desire to constantly evolve and achieve higher levels of success and fulfillment. In this response, I will elaborate on the importance of seeking personal and professional development and provide practical examples to illustrate its significance.

Personal Development:

Personal development focuses on enhancing various aspects of an individual's life, including their mindset, emotional intelligence, interpersonal skills, and overall well-being. Here are some practical examples of seeking personal development:

a) Mindset Growth: An individual may engage in activities such as reading personal development books, attending workshops or seminars, or participating in mindset coaching programs to cultivate a growth mindset. This helps them overcome self-limiting beliefs, embrace challenges, and view failures as learning opportunities.

b) Emotional Intelligence: Developing emotional intelligence involves understanding and managing one's own emotions and effectively relating to others. One can seek personal development by practicing self-reflection, seeking feedback, and participating in emotional intelligence workshops or training programs to improve their self-awareness, empathy, and relationship-building skills.

c) Well-being Enhancement: Seeking personal development in terms of well-being may involve adopting healthy habits, such as regular exercise, meditation, or mindfulness practices. It could also include attending personal wellness retreats or seeking the guidance of a life coach to create a balanced and fulfilling lifestyle.

Professional Development:

Professional development is essential for staying competitive in the rapidly evolving workplace and advancing one's career. It focuses on acquiring new skills, expanding knowledge in one's field, and fostering professional growth. Here are practical examples of seeking professional development:

a) **Skill Acquisition:** Professionals can pursue professional development by actively seeking opportunities to acquire new skills. This could involve attending industry conferences, enrolling in online courses, or participating in workshops to learn new technologies, methodologies, or leadership skills.

b) **Networking and Mentorship:** Building a strong professional network and seeking mentorship opportunities are vital for professional development. Attending industry events, joining professional associations, or actively engaging in networking platforms can provide valuable connections and insights.

Seeking out mentors who can offer guidance and support can accelerate professional growth.

c) Continuing Education: In rapidly evolving fields, continuous learning is crucial. Professionals can seek professional development by pursuing additional certifications or advanced degrees. This demonstrates a commitment to staying updated in their field and can open doors to new opportunities.

d) Leadership Development: Developing leadership skills is important for career advancement. Professionals can seek personal and professional development by participating in leadership training programs, taking on leadership roles in projects, or seeking mentorship from experienced leaders.

By actively seeking personal and professional development, individuals can unlock their full potential, adapt to changes, and stay ahead in their personal and professional lives. The examples provided demonstrate how seeking continuous growth can lead to improved skills, increased knowledge, and overall success in various areas of life. Embracing this mindset not only benefits individuals but also contributes to the growth and development of organizations and communities as a whole.

14.3 Embracing a Growth Mindset

Embracing a growth mindset is the foundation for continuous learning and growth. It is the belief that our abilities, intelligence, and talents can be developed through dedication, hard work, and a willingness to learn from our failures and setbacks. Individuals with a growth mindset perceive challenges as opportunities for growth, view effort as a necessary step toward mastery, and embrace feedback and criticism as valuable sources of improvement.

To better understand the concept of embracing a growth mindset, let's explore it through practical examples:

Challenges as Opportunities:

Someone with a growth mindset sees challenges as opportunities for personal development. They believe that with effort and perseverance, they can overcome obstacles and acquire new skills. For instance, imagine a student who struggles with math. Instead of avoiding the subject or believing they are inherently bad at it, they embrace the challenge, seek help from teachers or tutors, practice regularly, and gradually improve their math skills. They understand that their abilities can be developed through effort and dedication.

Effort and Persistence:

Individuals with a growth mindset recognize that effort and persistence are essential for success. They understand that mastery requires practice and are willing to put in the necessary work. For example, consider an aspiring musician who dreams of becoming proficient on a particular instrument. They devote regular time to practice, even when faced with difficult techniques or complex musical pieces. They understand that their progress may be gradual, but with each practice session, they move closer to their goal. They view mistakes and setbacks as learning opportunities and continue to put in the effort required to improve.

Embracing Feedback and Criticism:

A growth mindset involves embracing feedback and criticism as valuable tools for growth. Individuals with this mindset understand that feedback provides insight into areas where they can improve and refine their skills. For instance, let's say an employee receives constructive criticism about their presentation skills. Instead of feeling discouraged or defensive, they appreciate the feedback and use it to identify specific areas for improvement. They might seek additional resources, attend public speaking workshops, or practice in front of colleagues to enhance their skills. By embracing feedback, they continuously develop their abilities and become more effective in their role.

Learning from Failure:

Failure is an inevitable part of life, but individuals with a growth mindset see it as a stepping stone to success. They understand that failure provides valuable lessons and opportunities for growth. For example, an entrepreneur who experiences a business setback doesn't view it as a definitive failure. Instead, they analyze what went wrong, identify the lessons learned, and use that knowledge to pivot and improve their approach. They understand that setbacks are temporary and that resilience and adaptability are key to long-term success.

Embracing Continuous Learning:

A growth mindset is rooted in a love for learning and a belief that knowledge can be expanded throughout one's life. Those with this mindset actively seek out opportunities to learn and acquire new skills. They engage in self-study, take on new challenges, and pursue personal and professional development. For instance, a professional who wants to advance in their career may enroll in online courses, attend workshops, or seek mentorship opportunities to acquire new knowledge and skills. They understand that continuous learning not only expands their abilities but also opens doors to new opportunities.

In summary, embracing a growth mindset involves perceiving challenges as opportunities, valuing effort and persistence, embracing feedback and criticism, learning from failure, and actively pursuing continuous learning. By adopting this mindset, individuals can unlock their full potential, foster personal and professional growth, and overcome obstacles on their path to success.

CHAPTER FIFTEEN

Sustaining Success and Leaving a Legacy

15.1 Creating a Lasting Impact

Creating a lasting impact is a fundamental goal for individuals and organizations alike. It involves making meaningful contributions that endure beyond the present moment, leaving a positive mark on people's lives and the world as a whole. By focusing on sustaining success and leaving a legacy, individuals and organizations can adopt strategies and actions that have long-term effects. Let's explore this concept further and provide practical examples of creating a lasting impact.

Identify a Purposeful Vision:

To create a lasting impact, it is crucial to have a clear vision that aligns with your values and aspirations. A purposeful vision serves as a guiding principle and motivates you to pursue actions that will make a difference. For instance, Mahatma Gandhi had a vision of a free and independent India, which guided his nonviolent struggle for independence and inspired millions.

Engage in Sustainable Practices:

Sustainability is key to leaving a positive legacy for future generations. By adopting sustainable practices, individuals and organizations can minimize their negative impact on the environment and promote responsible resource management. An excellent example of sustainable practices is the introduction of renewable energy sources, such as solar panels or wind turbines, to reduce carbon emissions and combat climate change.

Invest in Education and Knowledge Sharing:

One of the most impactful ways to create a lasting impact is by investing in education and knowledge sharing. By empowering others with knowledge and skills, you contribute to their personal and professional growth, which can ripple through generations. Prominent philanthropist Bill Gates, through his foundation, has dedicated significant resources to education initiatives worldwide, providing access to quality education for millions of people.

Foster Social and Economic Development:

Creating a lasting impact involves actively working towards social and economic development. This can be achieved by promoting inclusive growth, reducing poverty, and fostering opportunities for marginalized communities. Muhammad Yunus, the founder of Grameen Bank, revolutionized microfinance by providing small loans to impoverished individuals, empowering them to start their own businesses and break the cycle of poverty.

Champion Social Justice and Equality:

To create a lasting impact, it is crucial to advocate for social justice and equality. By standing up against discrimination, oppression, and systemic injustices, individuals and organizations can contribute to a fairer society. The civil rights movement led by Martin Luther King Jr. fought for racial equality and played a significant role in shaping civil rights legislation and changing societal attitudes.

Support Sustainable Development Goals:

The United Nations Sustainable Development Goals (SDGs) provide a framework for addressing global challenges and creating a lasting impact. By aligning efforts with specific SDGs, individuals and organizations can contribute to the larger goal of sustainable development. For example, organizations like TOMS Shoes have integrated the SDG of "No Poverty" by donating a pair of shoes to a child in need for every pair purchased, addressing both poverty and access to education.

Inspire and Mentor Others:

Creating a lasting impact involves inspiring and mentoring others to reach their full potential. By sharing your experiences, knowledge, and lessons learned, you can empower individuals to overcome obstacles and achieve their goals. A notable example is Oprah Winfrey, who has used her platform to inspire millions through her talk show, philanthropy, and mentorship programs.

Preserve Cultural Heritage and Diversity:

Preserving cultural heritage and diversity is essential for creating a lasting impact. By valuing and safeguarding traditions, languages, and historical sites, we ensure that future generations can learn from and appreciate the richness of our shared humanity. UNESCO's World Heritage Sites, such as the Great Wall of China or the Pyramids of Egypt, are examples of efforts to preserve and protect cultural treasures for generations to come.

In conclusion, creating a lasting impact involves a combination of purposeful vision, sustainable practices, education, social justice advocacy, and mentorship. By engaging in these actions and supporting initiatives that align with your values, you can leave a positive legacy that transcends time and positively impacts individuals, communities, and the world.

15.2 Giving Back and Paying It Forward

Giving Back and Paying It Forward are two powerful concepts that go hand in hand, guided by the principle of "Sustaining Success and leaving a legacy." They involve the act of contributing to society and making a positive impact on the lives of others. By actively participating in these practices, individuals and organizations not only enhance their own success but also create a ripple effect that benefits the larger community. We will explore the essence of giving back and paying it forward, providing practical examples of how they can be implemented.

Giving back refers to the act of returning resources, whether it be time, money, skills, or knowledge, to the community or causes that have supported one's success. It involves a genuine desire to make a meaningful difference and create positive change. Giving back can take various forms, such as philanthropy, volunteering, mentoring, and supporting charitable organizations.

One practical example of giving back is philanthropy. Successful individuals or organizations may choose to donate a portion of their wealth to support causes they are passionate about. This could involve funding scholarships for underprivileged students, establishing grants for aspiring entrepreneurs, or contributing to research initiatives aimed at finding solutions to pressing global issues. For instance, Warren Buffett and Bill and Melinda Gates launched the Giving Pledge, a commitment by the world's wealthiest individuals to give away the majority of their wealth to address society's most pressing problems.

Another example of giving back is volunteering. This involves offering one's time and expertise to support organizations or projects that align with their values. For instance, a successful professional in the field of technology may volunteer to teach coding skills to disadvantaged youth, empowering them with valuable knowledge and opening doors of opportunity. Similarly, a retired doctor could volunteer at a free clinic, providing healthcare services to those who cannot afford it. Volunteering not only provides direct assistance but also inspires others to get involved, creating a positive domino effect.

Paying It Forward, on the other hand, takes the concept of giving back a step further. It involves not only reciprocating the support received but also actively empowering others to achieve their own success. Paying It Forward is about sharing knowledge, resources, and opportunities with others, with the belief that by investing in someone else's growth, we contribute to a stronger, more prosperous future for all.

An excellent example of paying it forward is mentorship. Successful individuals can act as mentors, sharing their wisdom and experiences with aspiring individuals in their field. By providing guidance, advice, and support, mentors can help others navigate challenges, make informed decisions, and unlock their full potential. This mentor-mentee relationship creates a cycle of continuous learning and growth, enabling the mentees to eventually become mentors themselves and pass on their knowledge to others.

Another example of paying it forward is creating opportunities for others. Successful entrepreneurs can invest in startup incubators or venture capital funds, supporting aspiring entrepreneurs with the necessary resources to turn their innovative ideas into thriving businesses. By providing access to funding, mentorship, and a supportive ecosystem, these entrepreneurs not only help others succeed but also foster innovation and economic growth in their communities.

In conclusion, giving back and paying it forward are essential practices that embody the principle of "Sustaining Success and leaving a legacy." By actively contributing to the betterment of society, individuals and organizations create a positive impact that extends far beyond their immediate sphere of influence. Whether through philanthropy, volunteering, mentorship, or creating opportunities, these acts of giving back and paying it forward empower others, inspire change, and contribute to a more prosperous and compassionate world.

15.3 Passing on Wisdom and Knowledge

Passing on wisdom and knowledge is a crucial aspect of sustaining success and leaving a lasting legacy. It involves sharing one's experiences, insights, and expertise with others, thereby empowering them to grow and make better decisions in their own lives and endeavors. This act of mentorship and knowledge transfer not only benefits the individuals involved but also contributes to the overall progress and development of society. In this response, I will elaborate on the importance of passing on wisdom and knowledge, along with practical examples to illustrate its impact.

a)		**Mentoring and Coaching:** One effective way to pass on wisdom and knowledge is through mentoring and coaching relationships. Experienced professionals or leaders can guide and support individuals who are starting their careers or pursuing specific goals. For instance, imagine a seasoned entrepreneur who mentors a young startup founder by sharing their experiences, providing advice on navigating challenges, and helping them develop essential business skills. Through this mentorship, the entrepreneur passes on their wisdom and knowledge, equipping the mentee with valuable insights to overcome obstacles and achieve success.

b) **Educational Institutions:** Schools, colleges, and universities play a vital role in passing on wisdom and knowledge to the next generation. Educators not only teach academic subjects but also impart valuable life skills and lessons. By creating an environment that fosters critical thinking, creativity, and collaboration, educational institutions enable students to acquire wisdom and knowledge beyond textbooks. For example, a history teacher might not only teach historical facts but also share stories of leaders who have made a significant impact on society, instilling valuable lessons about leadership, perseverance, and empathy.

c) Oral Tradition and Storytelling: Many cultures around the world have a rich tradition of passing down wisdom and knowledge through oral storytelling. Elders and community leaders share narratives, legends, and parables to impart moral lessons, cultural values, and practical advice. These stories serve as a bridge between generations, preserving the collective wisdom of the past and ensuring its continuity. For instance, indigenous tribes may pass on knowledge about the environment, traditional healing practices, or effective agricultural techniques through storytelling, ensuring that their wisdom is not lost over time.

d) Professional Networks and Communities: Engaging in professional networks and communities is another way to pass on wisdom and knowledge. These platforms bring together individuals with similar interests, experiences, or areas of expertise. Through discussions, workshops, conferences, and mentorship programs, professionals can exchange insights, share best practices, and learn from each other's successes and failures. For instance, in the field of technology, open-source communities allow developers to contribute their knowledge and collaborate on projects, thereby fostering continuous learning and innovation.

e) Publishing and Media: Books, articles, podcasts, and online platforms provide opportunities to pass on wisdom and knowledge to a broader audience. Experts, thought leaders, and individuals with unique experiences can share their insights, research findings, and practical advice through various mediums. For example, a renowned author may write a self-help book, offering guidance on personal growth and success strategies based on their own life journey. The dissemination of such knowledge through publishing and media channels allows a vast number of people to benefit and apply the wisdom shared.

In summary, passing on wisdom and knowledge is essential for sustaining success and leaving a legacy. Whether through mentoring, educational institutions, oral tradition, professional networks, or publishing, individuals can share their experiences, expertise, and insights to empower others. By doing so, they contribute to the growth and development of individuals, communities, and society as a whole.

ABOUT THE AUTHOR

Seth N. Taylor is a highly accomplished success coach and a prominent figure in the world of entrepreneurship. With an unwavering passion for personal development and a keen business acumen, Taylor has carved a remarkable path for himself and inspired countless individuals to unlock their true potential.

Born and raised in a small town, Taylor's journey to success was not without its fair share of challenges. Growing up, he faced financial hardships and limited opportunities, which fueled his determination to create a better life for himself and others. Armed with a relentless drive and a thirst for knowledge, he embarked on a journey of self-discovery and personal growth.

Taylor's early years were marked by various entrepreneurial ventures, where he honed his skills and gained valuable experience in business management. Through both successes and failures, he cultivated a deep understanding of the intricacies of entrepreneurship, ultimately transforming his insights into a powerful coaching methodology.

Driven by his desire to uplift and empower individuals, Taylor made it his mission to help others overcome obstacles and achieve their goals. He delved into the world of personal development, studying psychology, mindset strategies, and leadership principles. Combining his practical experience as an entrepreneur with his expertise in personal growth, he developed a unique coaching approach that encompasses both business strategies and personal transformation.

As a success coach, Taylor has guided countless individuals, from aspiring entrepreneurs to seasoned professionals, in achieving their dreams. He empowers his clients to identify their true passions, break through limiting beliefs, and create a roadmap for success. His coaching style is marked by a compassionate yet no-nonsense approach, fostering an environment of accountability and growth.

Taylor's impact extends beyond his one-on-one coaching sessions. He is a sought-after speaker and has delivered inspiring talks and workshops on various platforms. His ability to captivate audiences and deliver actionable insights has made him a respected figure in the personal development and entrepreneurial communities.

In addition to his coaching endeavors, Taylor is also a successful entrepreneur himself. He has founded and scaled multiple businesses, demonstrating his ability to translate his knowledge and expertise into tangible success stories. His entrepreneurial ventures span diverse industries, from technology startups to real estate investments, showcasing his versatility and adaptability in the business world.

Today, Seth N. Taylor continues to be a guiding light for individuals seeking personal and professional transformation. Through his coaching, writing, and speaking engagements, he inspires others to embrace their full potential, break free from limitations, and create lives of purpose and fulfillment. With a relentless commitment to empowering others,

Taylor is leaving an indelible mark on the world, one person at a time.

pg. 349

OTHER TITLES AND MATERIALS BY SETH

- **GETTING STARTED WITH LIFE:** The universal strategy for gaining early financial freedom

- **UNLOCKING THE SECRETS OF SUCCESS:** Mastering the 5 Habits of High Achievers

- **AMPLIFY YOUR BRAND:** Mastering Social Media Marketing for Rapid Growth

www.ingramcontent.com/pod-product-compliance
Lightning Source LLC
Chambersburg PA
CBHW052340220526
45465CB00003BA/894